# GRAMMAR
# MATTERS TOO
## TEACHER RESOURCE FILE

**Michael Ross**

Heinemann is an imprint of Pearson Education Limited, a company incorporated in England and Wales, having its registered office at Edinburgh Gate, Harlow, Essex, CM20 2JE. Registered company number: 872828

www.heinemann.co.uk

Heinemann is a registered trademark of Pearson Education Limited

Text © Pearson Education Limited 2008

First published 2008

12 11 10 09 08

10 9 8 7 6 5 4 3 2

British Library Cataloguing in Publication Data is available from the British Library on request.

ISBN 978 0 43522488 2

Designed and produced by Ken Vail Graphic Design

Word document layout by TAG Publishing Services

Cover design by Ken Vail Graphic Design

Cover illustration by Just for laffs (Martin Aston)

Printed by Ashford Colour Press

**Minimum system requirements**
PC
- Processor: 900mhz Intel Pentium III, (Vista 1GHz Pentium 4 or equivalent)
- OS: Windows 2000 Professional, Windows XP Professional, Windows Vista
- Memory: 256MB, (Vista Home Basic 512 MB, other Vista versions 1GB)
- Screen Resolution: 800x600
- Microsoft Word 2000 or above.

For further software support between the hours of 8.30–5.30 (Mon–Fri) please contact:

- Tel: 01865-888108
- Fax: 01865-314091
- Email: software.enquiries@pearson.com

**Acknowledgements**

Every effort has been made to contact copyright holders of material reproduced in this book. Any omissions will be rectified in subsequent printings if notice is given to the publishers.

Extract from *The Rough Guide to Books for Teenagers* by Nicholas Tucker (Rough Guides 2003). Copyright © Nicholas Tucker 2003. Reprinted with kind permission of Penguin; extract from *The Mind Game* by Hector MacDonald. Published by Penguin UK, 2000. Reprinted with kind permission of Conville and Walsh.

# GRAMMAR

# MATTERS TOO

## TEACHER RESOURCE FILE

# Contents

# Part C    Answers to Additional activities

# Part D    Additional resources

# Introduction

*Grammar Matters Too* comprises:

- Student Book
- Teacher's Resource File with CD-ROM (editable Word files of the TRF)
- Interactive CD-ROM.

The Teacher's Resource File has four functions:

- **Part A** provides sample answers to the Student Book activities.
- **Part B** consists of activities designed to extend students' thinking and understanding beyond what is covered in the Student Book.
- **Part C** provides answers to Part B.
- **Part D** includes a student self-assessment activity on grammar, plus some fact sheets that may help students gain an *overview* of some key concepts.

## Part B

The principles underlying the additional activities in Part B are:

- students should not be able to fill in 'blanks' in an unthinking way
- students are expected to work out which 'rule' applies in any given context (where 'rules' do exist)
- students are expected to be able to explain to fellow students how they made any decision or came to any conclusion
- students are expected to extend the range of strategies they can use in tackling any particular problem.

If students have to explain in detail their reasoning for placing an apostrophe of possession in a precise place, for example, there are many benefits:

- the act of explaining is a powerful way of clarifying one's own ideas
- other students can discuss how far the explanation is an accurate and helpful one
- the act of explaining requires students to think about their thinking, a form of *metacognition* which is essential to deeper learning and understanding.

In the additional activities a *single strategy* is provided which, if followed, will allow students to place the apostrophe of possession correctly every time. Rather than trying to remember a whole list of rules and exceptions, where possible the book provides an underlying principle or pattern.

There is therefore a strong emphasis in the additional activities on exploring the *logic and patterns* of the English language, rather than implying that it is all rather mysterious and irregular. The way word classes can be changed by using particular suffixes is just one example of how students can come to see that consistent patterns apply across many examples.

The 'true or false' section is intended as a light-hearted way of challenging misconceptions. Exploring *wrong answers* is a powerful way of reaching a deeper understanding.

Many students seem to think that English is not as 'solid' a subject as, for instance, Science. The additional resources should help to demonstrate some of the *logic* and some of the *patterns* embedded in the English language – too often invisible to them!

# Part A  Answers to Student Book activities

## Section 1   WORDS AND PHRASES

## Prefixes, stems and suffixes
### Student Book pages 6–9

### Activity 1

| Prefix | Stem | Suffix |
|--------|--------|--------|
| super | market | |
| tri | cycle | |
| anti | clockwise | |
| | remark | able |
| | amaze | ment |
| un | aware | |

*-wise* in *clockwise* is strictly a *combining form* rather than a *suffix*, but most teachers will probably want to credit students who include it!

### Activity 2

**Sample answers**

- My parents became **unfriendly** when I asked for some extra money.
- We were **unsure** how to follow the instructions.
- I had to stand in, and gave my performance completely **unrehearsed**.
- The teacher was **unsympathetic** when the student said she felt ill.

### Activity 3

| | | |
|---|---|---|
| **undercook** | *The food was clearly undercooked.* | |
| **incorrect** | *I knew that at least one of my answers was incorrect.* | |
| **prehistoric** | *The librarian bought books about prehistoric times.* | |
| **disadvantage** | *It was a disadvantage if you were the last to get changed.* | |
| **under-** | *prefix* | too little |
| **in-** | *prefix* | not |
| **pre-** | *prefix* | before |
| **dis-** | *prefix* | not |

### Activity 4

- I was **careful** when carrying the tray of drinks.
- His explanation was very **helpful**.
- The injury was the most **painful** of my life.
- Skating smoothly can look very **graceful**.
- It was a **careless** mistake.
- We all felt completely **helpless** under cross-examination.
- The operation was totally **painless**.
- The dancer's performance was unusually **graceless**.

**Note:** Changing from *-ful* to *-less* reverses the meaning.

### Activity 5

- We were **helped** onto the rowing boat.
- I like **helping** backstage.
- I could have **danced** all night.
- They were practically **dancing** up the aisle.

### Activity 6

| -ment | -ful | -ly | -ness | -ing |
|-------|------|-----|-------|------|
| entertainment refreshment | playful | playfully tidily loudly refreshingly | playfulness loudness tidiness | entertaining playing tidying refreshing |

Also **modernize** (for -ize).

### Activity 7

| Prefixes | Stems | Suffixes |
|----------|-------|----------|
| dis- in- re- un- | agree happy sincere turn | -ity -ly -able -ment -ness |

1  agreeable
2  agreement
3  disagree
4  disagreeable
5  happily
6  happiness
7  unhappy
8  unhappily
9  unhappiness
10  sincerity
11  sincerely
12  insincere
13  insincerity
14  insincerely
15  return
16  returnable

## Activity 8

1  Our class studied **global warming** today.

2  **Unfortunately**, we left the cake in the oven for too long and it didn't cook **properly**.

3  Helen couldn't hide her **excitement** when she **discovered** the truth.

4  On our **arrival**, the dog **immediately** ran to the door.

5  Our **teacher** told me to **simplify** my diagram, but I thought it was **amazing**.

6  The floor was really **dirty**, but we set about cleaning it **energetically**.

# Nouns

**Student Book pages 10–17**

## Activity 1

| People | Places | Things | Activities | States |
|--------|--------|--------|------------|--------|
| Visitors | centre world room | ocean view sharks turtles seahorses | games | Enjoyment |

## Activity 3

1  **Babies** enjoy hearing **stories** read to them.

2  The **heroes** of the **books** were police **chiefs**.

3  Close up **photos** of **mosquitoes** (or **mosquitos**) show how they bite.

4  Most successful **participants** in **quizzes** have a few good **guesses**.

5  Some **newspapers** like to report on the **lives** of the **wives** of football **players**.

6  The **thieves** stole all the **loaves** from the local supermarket **branches**.

**Note:** *quizzes* requires an extra z.

## Activity 4

1  The **women** and **men** were playing with their **children**. (-man *to* -men)

2  The **mice** were chasing the **lice**. (-ouse *to* -ice)

3  The **geese** were eating the bread at our **feet**. (-oo *to* -ee)

4  There are no **formulae** for the number of **antennae** and **vertebrae** in animals. (-a *to* -ae)

5  What **criteria** are used to tell the difference between normal events and strange **phenomena**? (-on *to* -a)

6  There are many different **species** of **deer** and **sheep**. (no change)

## Activity 5

| Category | Proper noun |
|----------|-------------|
| Country, nationality and/or language | Australia Japanese |
| Town or city | Bath Edinburgh |
| Name of person | Doctor Jones Jamie Oliver |
| Religion | Hinduism Christianity |
| Brand names | Pepsi Nike |
| Organisations | Oxfam Royal Mail |
| Calendar days, months and holidays | Halloween September |

## Activity 7

| Count nouns | Non-count nouns | |
|-------------|-----------------|---|
| egg | advice | excitement |
| book | anger | hay |
| computer | beef | luck |
| cow | bread | tennis |
| example | butter | |
| remark | | |

## Activity 8

**Possible answers**

● There are **fewer cars** on the road on Sunday mornings.

- I had **less money** for the trip than I had planned.
- There were **fewer problems** with the computer network.
- The pet shop had **fewer rabbits** than usual.
- There is **less traffic** on the road on Sunday mornings.

## Activity 9

### Possible answers

- There were **many cars** on the road on Monday morning.
- I didn't have **much money** left.
- There were **many problems** with the computer network.
- **Many rabbits** had escaped from the cage.
- There wasn't **much traffic** on the road on Sunday morning.

## Activity 10

- *smile*   *an expression of the face in which the corners of the mouth are turned up, usually expressing pleasure/amusement*
- *grin*   *a broad smile*
- *smirk*   *an unpleasant smile used because something bad has happened to someone else or after achieving a supposed advantage over someone else*

- The 'smirk' version is definitely suspicious and this person may not be trustworthy.
- The grin could be a cheeky grin, indicating probably harmless mischief.
- The smile hints at the most trustworthy person.

This activity is designed to promote discussion about nuances of meaning in words and the words authors use. There are no absolute right answers, but students should be aware of the underlying meanings in these words – *smirk* in particular.

## Activity 11

### Possible answers

- *mobs, yobs, gangs of youths* would suggest the author is trying to encourage a very negative attitude towards these young people.
- *youngsters, youths* would create a much more positive effect.

Some students may note that words like *hooded* and *loitered* may suggest an adult rather than young person's perspective, and a negative adult perception at that!

Definition of loiter: stand or wait around without a purpose.

## Activity 12

The waiter slipped on **the newly-mopped floor** and **the tray of freshly-prepared food** flew through the air. We saw **bits of trifle** land on **the hysterical woman**.

## Activity 13

| | | |
|---|---|---|
| active → activity | ~~e~~ + ity | **Pattern Aii** |
| advertise → advertisement | + **ment** | **Pattern Bi** |
| agile → agility | ~~e~~ + ity | **Pattern Aii** |
| argue → argument | ~~e~~ + ment | **Pattern Bii** |
| assess → assessment | + **ment** | **Pattern Bi** |
| conclude → conclusion | ~~de~~ + s + **ion** | **Pattern Cii** |
| create → creation | ~~e~~ + **ion** | **Pattern Ci** |
| decide → decision | ~~de~~ + s + **ion** | **Pattern Cii** |
| develop → development | + **ment** | **Pattern Bi** |
| engage → engagement | + **ment** | **Pattern Bi** |
| explain → explanation | ~~in~~ + na **tion** | |
| moral → morality | + **ity** | **Pattern Ai** |
| persuade → persuasion | ~~de~~ + s + **ion** | **Pattern Cii** |
| promote → promotion | ~~e~~ + **ion** | **Pattern Ci** |
| real → reality | + **ity** | **Pattern Ai** |

# Pronouns

**Student Book pages 18–23**

## Activity 1

1  Alice turned off the television because **she** was bored with what was on.

2  Wayne had scored three goals so **he** was made Man of the Match.

3  Pete and Ellie couldn't understand how **they** had lost the quiz.

4  You can recycle plastic and cardboard by placing **them** in the recycling bin.

## Activity 2

**Possible answer**

After what seemed like hours, a small castle appeared on the horizon. I had imagined it with stunning battlements and the sun beating down (on it). Instead, it was raining and the castle was hideous.

We entered (the castle). It was dark and gloomy. There was a stairway carved out of solid rock leading to a well, a water source deep inside the castle. The well would have been used when it was under siege.

**Note:** Various alternatives are possible.

## Activity 3

1  **I/He/She/We/They** heard the news today.

2  **He/She/You/They** should have listened to my advice.

3  **I/He/She/We/They** opened the letter, hoping for good news.

4  She told **me/him/her/us/them** the news.

5  The teacher recommended **me/him/her/us/you/them** for an award.

6  The manager used **me/him/her** as a substitute striker.

## Activity 4

1  That's not your book, it's **mine**.

2  You've had your meal. Now it's time for **ours**.

3  This is Daniel's t-shirt. **Hers** is still in the washing machine.

4  My team won last night. **Yours** lost.

5  Our bus has arrived. **Theirs** will arrive very soon.

## Activity 5

she = Angela

We = the company

We = the company

you = the reader

them = the crisps

you = the reader

## Activity 6

I switched the light on, dreading what I knew I would see. The vase my mum got for her 40th birthday from my nan was shattered into a million pieces. Kirsty and I looked at each other in horror. No one else seemed all that bothered. I attempted to sweep it up, but the feeling of dread was growing.

**Note:** Students will need to be alert and not change *her* 40th birthday to *my* 40th birthday.

Usually a first person account will give more sense of immediacy and involvement.

## Activity 8

Frank and Julia were reading in the garden. Their son John was mowing the lawn. **Frank** closed his book and asked **John** if he would like a drink. **John** said that was just what he needed, so **Frank** put his book down and made the drinks. When he returned, **John** and Julia were holding bags of grass. They put **the bags** down and Frank gave **the drinks** to them.

## Activity 9

1  The blazing hot sun forced me to slow down. (It)

2  I lost my favourite trainers. (them)

3  The books that I borrowed from the library were due back today. (They)

**4**   We watched <u>the large crashing waves</u>. (them)

**5**   I accidentally knocked <u>the blue vase</u> over. (it)

# Adjectives

## Activity 1

dark, gloomy, large, black, brilliant, golden, grand, old, wooden, tall, elegant, antique

**Note:** *antique* can be a noun but here it is an adjective.

## Activity 2

We're having a **fantastic** time, although the weather's been **terrible**. The sea was just **warm** enough for me to stay in for a **decent** swim, and Mark's been doing some surfing, which he says was **outstanding**. There was **heavy** rain on Sunday, but we spent our time in a **fascinating** place called Techniquest.

**Note:** Various alternatives are possible and they can reflect the more informal language of a postcard.

## Activity 3

Start your day with our **natural, health-boosting** breakfast smoothies. Made from **delicious** fruit, our smoothies are the most **nutritious** way to start your day.

**Note:** There are many alternatives possible but they should reflect the choices real advertisers would make in this context.

### Questions that will have been involved and can be made explicit

● Which adjective *matches which noun* best?

● Which adjectives are *most likely to convince* a customer to buy?

● Which combination of adjectives *works best together* at the start?

● Which adjectives would advertisers *actually choose*?

● Which adjectives give the most *positive and appealing image* of the product?

## Activity 4

### Issues that may arise

● Too many adjectives can clog up the writing rather than help a reader.

● Adjectives after the noun need to sound natural rather than forced.

● A variety of positions is preferable to a predictable pattern.

● The choice of adjective has to be appropriate and effective in the first place!

## Activity 5

### Discussion around some points that may arise

● The choice of *grimy* is precise and creates a clear mental picture. *cheap, red couch* provides an exact description of the couch.

● Students may criticise the use of fairly obvious words such as *small* and *black*. However, it should be stressed that sometimes a word such as *black* is just the right word and they should not force themselves to use unusual words every time.

● They may also be tempted to add more adjectives. Some writers argue that adjectives can clog up a text and that careful choice of verbs is more crucial to successful writing. *family, pushchair* and *woman* have no adjectives, which adds to the variety rather than undermining it.

● All the adjectives come before the nouns they modify, except for *baking* (it = the weather). The student might be encouraged to vary the positioning of adjectives more.

**Note:** *swinging* is being used as an adjective in this passage. It can be referred to as a modifier.

## Activity 6

**Comparatives:** <u>Faster</u> than a shuttle take-off, <u>speedier</u> than a Ferrari and with <u>more</u> lift than a plane

**Note:** *lift* is a noun; *more* is the comparative of *much* here

**Superlatives:** The UK's <u>most thrilling</u> theme park! Colossus, Nemesis, Inferno and Stealth – Europe's <u>fastest</u> and <u>tallest</u> rollercoaster.

## Activity 7

**1**  My old bedroom was **smaller** than the one I'm in now.

**2**  His spelling is **more accurate** than mine.

**3**  Be **stricter** when training your dog.

**4**  The book was **more interesting** than I thought.

**5**  The new building was **more spacious**.

## Activity 8

**1**  It was the **worst** meal I had ever eaten.

**2**  The final book in the trilogy was by far the **best**.

**3**  That was the **most exciting** game I have ever watched.

**4**  They were the **narrowest** lanes I've had to cycle through.

**5**  Waiting at the airport was the **most mind-numbing** experience I have ever had.

## Activity 10

Add -al to the noun. If the noun ends in e, drop the e.

## Activity 11

Add -ing to the verb. If the verb ends in e, drop the e.

# Verbs

**Student Book pages 32–39**

## Activity 1

**1**  On Saturday, Yasmeen <u>went</u> to the bookshop.

**2**  The bookshop <u>was</u> always busy on a Saturday.

**3**  The shop assistant <u>smiled</u> at Yasmeen from behind the counter.

**4**  Yasmeen <u>asked</u> the shop assistant for a particular book.

**5**  The shop assistant <u>had</u> a good knowledge of the bookshop.

## Activity 2

**1**  Joe <u>wonders</u> what it is like to be a famous footballer.

**2**  My brother <u>plays</u> the drums for a rock band.

**3**  It <u>was</u> a really good film.

**4**  Climbing is what Stacey <u>likes</u> to do at the weekend.

**5**  I sometimes wish we <u>had</u> more sunshine.

**Note:** Many alternatives are possible here.

## Activity 3

**Grumpy version:**

Mrs Green **stormed** into the bakery and **slammed** the door. The baker **glared** at Mrs Green and **barked**, 'What would you like?'

Mrs Green **screeched**, 'Three fruit scones.'

The baker **threw** the fruit scones into a paper bag, and Mrs Green **banged** the money on the counter.

**Friendly version:**

Mrs Green **strolled** into the bakery and **closed** the door. The baker **smiled** at Mrs Green and **asked**, 'What would you like?'

Mrs Green **replied**, 'Three fruit scones.'

The baker **placed** the fruit scones into a paper bag, and Mrs Green **put** the money on the counter.

## Activity 4

**1**  You <u>can join</u> the team.

**2**  I <u>will write</u> my postcards tomorrow.

**3**  Hannah <u>might leave</u> the party early.

**4**  Chris <u>has tidied</u> his bedroom.

**5**  I <u>may finish</u> the book before you.

**6**  I <u>do know</u> the rules of football.

**7**  My friend <u>has moved</u> to a different class.

**8**  The band <u>was playing</u> well.

**9**  I <u>could have solved</u> that puzzle.

**10**  Mrs Tulip <u>could have been</u> our teacher.

## Activity 5

| Verb phrase | Auxiliary verb/s | Main verb |
|---|---|---|
| can join | can | join |
| will write | will | write |
| might leave | might | leave |
| has tidied | has | tidied |
| may finish | may | finish |
| do know | do | know |
| has moved | has | moved |
| was playing | was | playing |
| could have solved | could have | solved |
| could have been | could have | been |

## Activity 6

I **might** go see that film this weekend. I **will** look on the internet and see if there are any reviews. That **could** tell me if it's worth watching. If I do see a good review, I **can** text you and we **could** go to the cinema together.

## Activity 7

**1**   Would you like some orange juice?

**2**   I have already watched that film.

**3**   Could we go somewhere else?

**4**   I had completely forgotten that.

## Activity 8

**1**   Gemma **throws** the ball to Sandy. (present time)

**2**   I **will go** shopping with Dad. (future time)

**3**   I **was** happy about being selected for the team. (past time)

**4**   I **left** for school as the downpour started. (past time)

**5**   The Earth **travels** around the Sun. (present time)

**6**   They **stayed** in the park all day. (past time)

**7**   Ray **is playing** on his computer. (present time)

**8**   My father **teaches** in a secondary school. (present time)

## Activity 9

Alton Towers **is** full of children. There **are** children everywhere. Everywhere you **look** there **is** an overexcited child screaming happily with the thought of all the fun contained in one park. The sweet stalls, covered in bags of candyfloss and other such brightly coloured delights, **are** heaving with hordes of sweet-toothed children. The ornament stalls **are** also packed.

**Note**

● *overexcited* is an adjective in this context

● *covered* is an -*ed* participle in this context.

## Activity 10

Everyone was expecting me to have a party. But I **hadn't** even asked my mum **at that stage/ at that point/then**. I thought she **would** probably say yes so I **decided** I **would** ask her **that** night.

I was going to invite my two best friends: Mandy and Suzy. I **decided** I **would** tell them about the party **the next day**.

## Activity 11

The operator – sitting in a glass cabin at one end of the crusher – *pressed* a button and there was a great belch of black smoke. The shelves *closed in* on the car like a monster insect folding in its wings. There was a grinding sound as the car *was crushed* until it was no bigger than a rolled-up carpet. Then the operator *threw* a gear and the car *was squeezed* out, metallic toothpaste *being chopped up* by a hidden blade. The slices *tumbled on* to the ground.

## Activity 12

| | |
|---|---|
| allow**ed** | allow**ing** |
| believ~~e~~**ed** | believ**eing** |
| brak~~e~~**ed** | brak**eing** |
| manag~~e~~**ed** | manag**eing** |
| den**ied** | deny**ing** |
| climb**ed** | climb**ing** |
| happen**ed** | happen**ing** |
| listen**ed** | listen**ing** |

## Activity 13

disappear, reappear, disappoint, reappoint, disassemble, preassemble, reassemble, photocopy, recopy, research, preview, review

### Possible subjects

- CDT for *disassemble, preassemble, reassemble*
- English and Drama for *review* (books, plays, etc.)
- Geography for *disappear, reappear* (underground rivers, etc.)
- History for *reappoint* when referring to a person regaining a position

# Adverbs

**Student Book pages 40–43**

## Activity 1

1   Alex was waiting <u>there</u>.
2   Nadine thought <u>carefully</u> about the question.
3   We planned to meet <u>today</u>.
4   Charlotte sang <u>confidently</u> at the karaoke.
5   Kamal wrote his letter <u>very</u> <u>neatly</u>.

## Activity 2

For one thing, it was lighter than all the others he had come across. <u>Far</u>, <u>far</u> lighter. This was <u>definitely</u> no ordinary tin of beans or soup or stewed steak or curried chicken or macaroni cheese. This was a tin which felt <u>so</u> light that it could <u>almost</u> have been empty. But despite being <u>so</u> light, it <u>definitely</u> had something inside it. Fergal knew that for certain. He could tell that <u>quite</u> <u>clearly</u>.

## Activity 3

### Possible answer

I was **particularly** interested in the new music download system. **Essentially** it was **extremely** easy to use, and you could **instantly** choose what you **specifically** wanted.

## Activity 4

### Possible answer

The manager had enthusiastically agreed to hold the party in the function room. She cheerfully walked towards the round table in the centre of the room. Quickly and efficiently she took orders. A party of twelve was already singing merrily.

## Activity 5

### Possible answer

I *got up* from my bed <u>sleepily</u>. <u>Foolishly</u>, *I* had left it <u>too</u> *late* as usual. I *searched* <u>frantically</u> for my school uniform, *finding* it <u>eventually</u> in various <u>extremely</u> *strange* places. After <u>rapidly</u> *eating* my breakfast, I left the house and ran to catch the bus.

   <u>Curiously</u>, the bus stop *was* <u>unusually</u> *quiet*. I <u>suddenly</u> *realised* the reason. It was a school closure day.

Note: *Curiously* is another way of saying *It was curious that …*

Adverbs at the start of sentences are often difficult to match.

## Activity 7

- necessary   $y \rightarrow i + \mathbf{ly}$
- terrible   ~~le~~ + $\mathbf{ly}$
- true   ~~e~~ + $\mathbf{ly}$
- whole   ~~e~~ + $\mathbf{ly}$

# Prepositions

**Student Book pages 44–47**

## Activity 1

My day started **at** 6 o'clock. I made some sandwiches **for** myself and collected my bike **from** the shed. I rode **to** school, avoiding the route **across** the dual carriageway and instead went **over** the bridge. I arrived just **before** the coach left, leaving my bike **beside** the school office.

## Activity 2

**Sample sentences**

- **At** the weekend I'm going fishing.
- I'll see you tomorrow **before** lessons start.
- **Between** breakfast and eight o'clock I had to finish all my homework.
- You need to be at the station **by** eight o'clock.
- **During** August we went on holiday.
- She'll be away **for** two weeks.
- We can meet up any time **from** lunchtime onwards.
- The repair will be ready **in** two weeks.
- We have a special celebration **on** May Day.
- **Over** the weekend I'm visiting my relations.
- It was well **past** my younger brother's bedtime.
- It's been fairly dry **since** the spring.
- We played football outside **until** it was nearly night time.

## Activity 6

This implies that no dogs have passed this point. As it stands, it is a statement of fact about what has happened up to now, using the past tense of the verb *to pass*.

What is intended is the preposition *past* meaning *beyond*:

Take the first door on the left past (beyond) the library.

**No dogs past this point** would mean:

Do not bring your dog(s) past (beyond) this sign.

# Section 2 SENTENCES

## What is a sentence?
**Student Book pages 48–49**

### Activity 1

**1** They **are** big and they are clever! *Yes*

**2** Dreamy white chocolate *No verb, no full stop: no*

**3** <u>Check out</u> our new healthy range. *Yes*

**4** Milk chocolate with gold honeycomb centre *No verb, no full stop: no*

**5** <u>**Do**</u> you **dare** to whizz, loop and twist on a journey of terror**?** *Yes*

**6** <u>How</u> about **trying** our spicy meat pizza**?** *Yes*

**7** Roly Poly Coaster *No verb, no full stop: no*

**8** <u>**Go**</u> round the bend! *Yes*

**9** <u>**Fly**</u> off the handle! *Yes*

**10** The crumbliest flakiest milk chocolate *No verb, no full stop: no*

### Activity 2

**1** <u>Everyone</u> **likes** a challenge.

**2** <u>**Use**</u> in a well-ventilated area.

**3** <u>**Enjoy!**</u>

**4** <u>Thousands</u> of sports fans **let out** a miserable cheer yesterday.

**5** <u>We</u> **will match** any price.

**6** <u>**Repeat**</u>, please.

**7** <u>My</u> side of the story **is** really simple.

**8** <u>**Buy**</u> now!

**9** <u>On</u> the morning of 25 February we **left** the city.

**10** <u>**Win!**</u>

## Kinds of sentence
**Student Book pages 50–51**

### Activity 1

**1** **Statements**

- Grandma's tiny face still bore the same foul and furious expression it had always had.
- Her eyes, no bigger now than little keyholes, were blazing with anger.
- And by golly she was.
- When she was no bigger than a cigarette, Mrs Kranky made a grab for her.
- But she calmed down quite quickly.
- George didn't say a word.

**Questions**

- 'How d'you think I feel?'
- How would you feel if you'd been a glorious giant a minute ago and suddenly you're a miserable midget?
- 'Where've you gone?'
- 'Where've you got to?'
- 'How can I find you?'

**Exclamations**

- 'She's still getting smaller!'
- 'I can hardly see her as it is!'
- 'I've lost her!'
- 'She's gone!'
- 'She's disappeared completely!'

**Note:** strictly these are *statements* with *exclamation marks*.

**2** **What do the questions and exclamations tell us about the relationship between Grandma, Mr Kranky and Mrs Kranky?**

- **'I *must* stop her!' Mrs Kranky wailed. 'I can hardly see her as it is!'**

- **'Where is she?' cried Mrs Kranky. 'I've lost her!'**
  Mrs Kranky's early questions and exclamations suggest she is very upset and disturbed about Grandma getting smaller and smaller. The exclamations suggest desperation and even panic.

- **'She was a bit of a nuisance around the house, wasn't she?'**
  Her final question suggests she will very quickly get used to the idea of Grandma not being there.

- **'She's still going!' shouted Mr Kranky gleefully. 'She's still getting smaller!'**
  Mr Kranky's 'exclamations' are in a completely different tone. He seems delighted that Grandma is steadily vanishing.

**3** **Imagine that the next thing George does is make a statement sentence. What might it be?**
I think my medicine was more powerful and magical than I'd realised.

# Simple sentences
**Student Book pages 52–55**

## Activity 1

**Possible answers**
1   The kite flew.
2   The river meandered.
3   I escaped.
4   Dad laughed.
5   The horse galloped.

## Activity 2

**Possible answers**
1   The football players **ran** onto the pitch.
2   The front door **opened** slowly.
3   Ravi didn't **believe** vampires were real.
4   The firework **blazed** in the sky.
5   The cottage **was covered** in snow.
6   The fans **cheered** loudly.
7   The firemen **put out** the fire.

8   The book **was** really exciting.

## Activity 4

1   The horse ran out of the stable.
2   Alice kicked the football.
3   The car reversed into the parking space.
4   London is a big city.
5   I accidentally threw the ball into the greenhouse.

## Activity 5

**Possible answers**
1   **Everyone** was busy tidying the house.
2   **The chandelier** crashed onto the floor.
3   **My sister** wanted me to go to the cinema last night.
4   **The sun** blazed down on the desert.
5   **Music** was playing really loudly.

## Activity 6

**The driver** crossed the line in first place. **The crowd** cheered with delight. **A trophy** was given to the driver for his victory. **Journalists** scrambled to get an interview with him.

## Activity 7

At the weekend we went to the Natural History Museum. There was plenty to see there. My favourite thing to visit was the dinosaur gallery. It was absolutely fascinating. All around there were lots of dinosaur skeletons. The Tyrannosaurus Rex's skeleton was gigantic! I bet it would have been terrifying to come across a real one. Now I can imagine what the people in *Jurassic Park* felt like!

## Activity 8

1   It *is* a really good film.
2   The thunder *rumbled* loudly.
3   I *was expecting* you to call.
4   Experiments in science lessons *can be* fun.
5   Some television programmes *are* really interesting.
6   Neither Lucy nor Fiona *plays* the clarinet.

**7** The footballer who played in all the matches *won* the award.

# Checking agreement
**Student Book pages 56–57**

## Activity 1

**1** We **were** watching a film at the cinema.

**2** They **were** in the library when we found them.

**3** I **was** playing my guitar with my friends.

**4** You **were** looking really embarrassed.

**5** Billy **was** late for his lesson.

## Activity 2

**1** The book that I was given by my parents **was** very good.

**2** My cousins Ros and Melissa **were** dancing to the music.

**3** The favourite of all Richard's hobbies **is** athletics.

**4** My parents, who aren't mad at me anymore, **are** taking me to the cinema.

**5** The plates, which crashed on the floor, **were** brand new.

**6** Sam, who came shopping with us, **was** really good company.

**7** Everyone, except Sarah and Maya, **was** going on the school trip.

# Object, Complement and Adverbial
**Student Book pages 58–59**

## Activity 1

**1** Mary dusted <u>the shelves</u>.

**2** Take <u>a break</u>.

**3** In October, I will celebrate <u>my thirteenth birthday</u>.

**4** The next issue of the magazine will have <u>more great bands</u>.

Note that the object can be replaced by a pronoun such as: *it, them.*

## Activity 2

**Possible answers**

**1** The chef prepared <u>four courses</u>.

**2** I photographed <u>elephants and giraffes</u> at the zoo.

**3** I would like <u>a new bicycle</u> for my birthday.

**4** In the newsagent's shop I bought <u>a newspaper</u>.

## Activity 3

**1** The food tasted <u>delicious</u>.

**2** She seemed <u>a bit tired</u>.

**3** Their team were <u>the winners</u>.

**4** Owen is <u>my best friend</u>.

**5** The table looked <u>rather dirty</u>.

**6** The pudding smelled <u>wonderful</u>.

## Activity 4

**1** His brother cycled <u>from home</u>.

**2** Charlie played the piano <u>very well</u>.

**3** Ewan laughed <u>vigorously</u>.

**4** We played basketball <u>until dinnertime</u>.

**5** My best friend called me <u>this morning</u>.

# Section 3   BUILDING SENTENCES

## Building simple sentences
**Student Book page 60**

### Activity 1

**Possible answers**

1   **The grandfather clock** was ticking loudly.

2   **The science teacher** walked into the classroom.

3   I like **many types of music**.

## Building noun phrases
**Student Book page 61**

'Boo!'

'Don't scare me like that,' hissed Dan.

'Why?' teased Alice. 'Are you scared? It's only an empty house.'

Thunder rumbled in the **threatening, lowering sky**.

Dan and Alice looked uneasily at the **mysterious, unlit house**. It stood at the top of a hill. They crept closer. There was no turning back now.

They reached the **jagged gate, entwined with nettles**. A **black cat** ran past, making Alice jump.

'Who's scared now?' joked Dan, nervously.

## Clauses
**Student Book pages 62–63**

### Activity 1

● **Examples of simple sentences**

The new boy <u>was surrounded</u> by a crowd of first years.

He <u>was</u> a big broad-shouldered lad with sun-tanned face and dark curly hair.

● **Examples of multiple sentences**

He <u>was dressed</u> in a fancy pullover and brown corduroys and he <u>was wearing</u> a tie.

The first years <u>seemed to be enjoying</u> his company, because they <u>were laughing</u> and <u>skipping</u> about him like a pack of playful dogs.

## Compound sentences
**Student Book pages 64–65**

### Activity 1

1   Shreena could spend her pocket money now **or** could save it for a rainy day.

2   I get the bus to school **but** I would rather ride my bike.

3   I sing lead vocal for the band **and** I play the guitar.

4   There are plenty of recycling facilities out there, **but** not everyone recycles.

5   You could take the stairs **or** you could take the escalator.

6   The house has three bedrooms **and** it has a garden.

7   I wanted to go swimming **but** the pool was closed.

8   Sami is good at science **and** he is good at art.

### Activity 2

I went to the zoo with my mum, dad and little brother Zach. We went straight to the monkey enclosure because monkeys are Zach's favourite. I was desperate to go to see the lions, but Mum and Dad said we should keep Zach happy. I didn't spend much time with the lions, but it was still a great trip. I can't wait until we go again.

# Connectives

## Activity 1

**Possible answers**

1    The café was closed **so** we went to the pizza place instead.

2    My mum was angry **because** my music was loud.

3    You can have some ice cream **if** you finish your vegetables.

4    Jan and Philip were gossiping **while** the teacher was talking.

5    It has been raining, **although** it is still pretty warm.

6    You won't be going out **until/unless** you have finished your homework.

7    Our goalkeeper isn't here, **so** we could use someone else for now.

8    Julian got a really good mark **although** he had arrived late for the test.

9    We put the tomato on the pizza base, **then** we add the cheese.

10    We got a recycling bin **after** we started collecting glass and paper.

## Activity 2

1    We went to the pizza place instead **because** the cafe was closed.

2    My music was loud **so** my mum was angry.

3    **If** you finish your vegetables you can have some ice cream.

4    **While** the teacher was talking, Jan and Philip were gossiping.

5    It is still pretty warm **although** it has been raining.

6    **Until/Unless** you have finished your homework, you won't be going out.

7    We could use someone else for now **as** our goalkeeper isn't here.

8    **Although** he had arrived late for the test, Julian got a really good mark.

9    We add the cheese **after** we put the tomato on the pizza base.

10    **After** we started collecting glass and paper, we got a recycling bin.

**Note:** All these sentences can be reversed, but in some cases the connective needs to be changed. Some connectives will only work in the middle; some can also go at the start of the sentence. All the answers to Activity 1 and Activity 2 are complex sentences.

# Complex sentences

## Activity 1

1    The goalkeeper got struck by the ball **when** the striker took his shot. *f*

2    I wouldn't speak to him **until** he apologised. *j*

3    I could stay at your house **if** my mum says that's OK. *b*

4    We're not going to make it in time **unless** you hurry up. *a*

5    I have been feeling stronger **since** starting karate classes. *c*

6    Ravi told me a joke **because** I was upset. *i*

7    I decided it was time to tidy my bedroom **when** I couldn't open my wardrobe door. *h*

8    Mum made me fill in a calendar **after** I forgot Dad's birthday. *d*

9    I looked at the horizon **while** swimming. *g*

10    We could stay in and watch a film **although** it is a nice day outside. *e*

# More about clauses

## Activity 1

1    I was walking up the stairs **when** I tripped over.

2    James counted to ten **while** Maya hid under the table.

3    I was with my friends **although** I felt really bored.

4    It was my birthday **so** we went to Alton Towers.

5    Will told us a secret **which** made us gasp.

## Activity 3

Dear Graham,

**Since** I have always been interested in unusual animals, I think I would like to keep an unusual pet at home. **Although** I already have a cat and a goldfish, I would like to keep more animals. I live in a three-bedroom house with my mum and young brother **so** it isn't too crowded.

I would like to know what you recommend, **though** I am thinking of a snake or scorpion.

I look forward to hearing from you.

Yours sincerely,

Tom, age 13

# Sentences and how to stop them

### Student Book pages 72–73

## Activity 1

Haverstock <u>was</u> barely a village. It <u>was</u> a small and isolated place with a church, a shop, a few houses, a telephone box and a crossroads. There <u>was</u> a dried-up duck pond near the graveyard, with an old, ruined stocks by it.

Charlotte <u>reached</u> into her pocket and <u>felt</u> for her phone. It <u>wasn't</u> there. It <u>must have fallen out</u> when she <u>had been running</u>. She <u>stopped</u> by the telephone box. Maybe she <u>ought to call</u>, to tell someone where she <u>was</u>, just in case. But then she <u>realised</u> that the few coins she <u>had were</u> of no use; the payphone only <u>took</u> silver. She <u>didn't</u> even <u>think</u> to reverse the charges. She just <u>hurried</u> on.

## Activity 2

She walked on. It was a cold but clear country night. Pale moonlight showed the way. Her footsteps echoed and seemed at times to be pursuing her, then at other times to be slightly ahead of her, as though she was following them. Hedges and brambles lined the fields, and twisted thorn trees writhed as if locked in pain. A faint, whispering breeze blew, full of murmuring.

# Looking at a text

### Student Book pages 74–75

## Activity 1

1  • One question: *Can you believe it's happened again?*

   • One statement: (*any complete sentence except the question*)

   • One example of a simple sentence: *This will sound very familiar.*
   *There is an alternative.*

   • One example of a compound sentence: *You've got to get somewhere urgently but your car doesn't start.*
   *Normally you'd start shouting, crying or kicking the car.*

2  Explain why you think the author starts the advertisement with a question. *To engage the reader. To encourage the reader to remember when they have been in a similar situation in their car.*

3  Explain why you think the author starts the main text with a statement. *Following on from the question, the copywriter wants readers to identify themselves with this situation – giving the sentence the status of a statement of fact.*

4  Explain why you think the author chose to place the shortest sentence at exactly the point it is in the advertisement. *This is the punch-line of the first section of the advertisement. The <u>problem</u> has been clearly stated – now comes the <u>solution</u> from Rapid Rescue.*

## Activity 2

1  What kinds of sentences are being used? *questions, directives, statements, directives with exclamation marks*

**3** Choose the sentence that you think is the most powerful. Be prepared to explain your choice. *Students need to make a case for the sentence they choose. It is likely to be linked to a strong challenge to the reader's present behaviour. It may be a rhetorical question like the first sentence, or a directive like the second, or a statement like the third. The aim is for students to discuss the link between choice of words, choice of sentence type and the impact on the reader.*

**4** Find examples of the following:
- a short sentence with a short dramatic message: *Cease this madness!*
- exclamations to add to the impact and emotion: *Don't do this to yourselves, people! Cease this madness!*

**Note:** strictly these are directives with exclamation marks.

- first person plural pronoun to involve the reader: **We** all know the risks, but **we** shrug our shoulders and carry on blocking up our arteries and reducing the blood supply to our heart. **We** all know what's healthy and what's not, so let's do something about it.
- second person pronoun to involve the reader: *How many of **you** have been to a fast food restaurant this week? Some of **you** reading this article, right now, could die as a result of your eating habits.*
- use of logical connectives to explain where the argument is leading: *so, so*
- use of questions to involve the reader: *How many of you have been to a fast food restaurant this week? Why not go to a healthier food store? Why not bring your own sandwiches?*

# Section 4    PARAGRAPHS AND WHOLE TEXTS

## Your writing
### Student Book pages 78–81

### Activity 1

**1** The paragraph that tells you:
- about the road network = 1
- how easy it is to make friends = 2
- how far people help each other = 2
- what other people know about this place = 3
- what the writer's overall feelings are about the place = 3
- where the place is = 1

**2** Labels to each paragraph:
- opinions about the place = 3
- the people = 2
- the place = 1

**3** The paragraphs are arranged logically:
- setting the scene – letting the reader know where the author is writing about
- going into more detail – saying what it's like to live there
- challenging misconceptions – exploring what other people think/assume about the place.

### Activity 2

**1** If you are looking for things to do in the morning … A

**2** The first thing you need to know is where you can stay. C

**3** What most people consider to be the centre and heart of … is …. B

# Section 5  PUNCTUATION

## Capital letters
**Student Book pages 82–83**

### Activity 1

For (A) the school trip last year, I (D) went to the Millennium Centre (B) in Cardiff (B) to see the play version of Dickens's (B) Nicholas Nickleby. (G) This (A) version was written by David Edgar, (B) and it was originally performed by the RSC (F) in Stratford-upon-Avon. (B) One (A) critic said, 'This (E) tremendous Dickensian (C) production was greeted by a spontaneous standing ovation.'

### Activity 2

My mum and I went to Glasgow during the half-term holiday to see Grandad. We haven't seen him in ages. I love hearing his Scottish accent.

We took the train from Bristol and travelled steadily north. The journey took ages. I read *Harry Potter and the Philosopher's Stone* by JK Rowling to pass the time. We eventually arrived there in the early evening. When we got to grandad's house, Mum called Dad to say we had arrived safely.

## Full stops, question marks and exclamation marks
**Student Book pages 84–85**

### Activity 1

The teacher asked me if I had read the latest Philip Pullman novel.

I asked, 'Which one is that?'

She named the book and I replied, 'Yes, I read it as soon as it came out. What a fantastic read!'

I asked if she'd enjoyed reading it.

She said yes, and added, 'Do you think the same central character might be used again?'

I said I thought it would be a good idea, but asked if this could go on much longer.

She replied, 'With a writer of that talent, there's no doubt that anything is possible, don't you think?'

I agreed with her, exclaiming, 'No doubt at all!'

## Commas
**Student Book pages 86–87**

### Activity 1

1  I would like some bananas, apples, oranges and mangoes. *A*

2  Alison asked, 'What if they don't turn up?' *C*

3  It was a cold, wet, windy, miserable day. *B*

4  We visited places in England, Scotland, Ireland and Wales. *A*

5  'That's really kind of you,' I replied. *C*

6  Secretly, she crept into the room. *D*

7  'I went to her house,' I said quickly, 'to apologise.' *C*

### Activity 2

1  After that terrible result, the coach changed his training methods. (Reason a)

2  The referee, having looked at the action replay, decided not to award a penalty. (Reason c)

3  I rushed into the house, took off my shoes, hung up my jacket and sat down. (Reason b)

4  The result, when the whistle was finally blown, was a complete surprise. (Reason c)

5  Before leaving home(,) I tried out my speech. (Reason a)

## Apostrophes
**Student Book pages 88–91**

### Activity 1

1  I **didn't** manage to see the film last night, so **I'll** have to watch it next time **it's** on.

**2**  I **don't** think **you're** going to make it in time for the kick-off.

**3**  If I **can't** open this jar, I **shan't** be having jam on my toast.

**4**  **It's** been really sunny today, so **we've** made a picnic for lunch.

## Activity 2

**1**  It **is** time to get up.

**2**  I **had** expected you to be more enthusiastic.

**3**  **There is** a programme on television tonight that **you would** enjoy.

**4**  **Who would** have predicted that result?

**5**  **You have** helped me make a good choice: it **has** been well worth reading that book.

## Activity 3

**1**  Emily's jumper is red.

**2**  We are going to Jamie's house this afternoon.

**3**  Dad's headache isn't getting any better.

**4**  I saw the article in yesterday's newspaper.

**5**  Last night's dinner was delicious.

**6**  We did some creative writing in Friday's lesson.

## Activity 4

**1**  The magicians' tricks were fantastic! (**Note:** there were three magicians.)

**2**  My aunt likes writing children's stories.

**3**  Dad tried to find a present for Mum in the women's clothing department.

**4**  The judges' decision was final. (**Note:** there were four judges.)

## Activity 5

- Classic songs from the 1960s
- DVDs for £10
- Tomatoes, Potatoes, Bananas

## Activity 6

**Idea 1:** Before long, Spider Man suits will exist that could make some young people's dreams come true. It will be possible to climb a skyscraper's vertical face.

**Idea 2:** Tiny hooks can be built into gloves so that they can grip a smooth surface such as glass. Each glove's designed to hold a man's weight or a woman's weight. Two gloves could even hold two men's weight or two women's weight!

**Idea 3:** It's an idea based on a type of lizard called a *gecko*. A gecko's hand has tiny hairs that help it cling to a smooth surface. But don't rush out and try to buy one just yet. They might be in the shops in ten years' time.

# Colons and semi-colons
### Student Book pages 92–93

## Activity 1

**1**  As CP Scott said: comment is free but facts are sacred. *C*

**2**  I decided not to argue: the friendship was more important. *B*

**3**  My parents' shopping list included: a barbecue, an outdoor table, some firelighters and some sort of parasol for shelter from the sun. *A*

**4**  The instructions fixed to the back of the rowing boat read: no changing positions in the boat when away from the shore. *C*

**5**  This lesson may be interrupted: there is a visitor due. *B*

**6**  To make a kite you need: a light frame, some light but strong fabric and a long piece of string. *A*

## Activity 2

**1**  He enjoys: playing the trombone; football and rugby; and any kind of martial art. *A*

**2**  I eat meat; he is a vegetarian. *C*

**3**  The directions were clear; but the mist made them impossible to follow. *C*

**4** Our team all had identical smart football kit; their team were wearing t-shirts of roughly the same shade of green. *C*

**5** I ran to the bus stop; I jumped on the bus; I got off in town; and I ran to the station. *B*

**6** You may use the sports hall on condition that you: remove outdoor shoes; look after the equipment; pay for any breakages; and leave the place tidy. *A*

**7** The students behaved in different ways: some chatted to their neighbour; some read a book; while others got ahead with their homework. *A*

# Speech marks and inverted commas

**Student Book pages 94–97**

## Activity 1

**1** 'What time are we meeting today?'

**2** 'I found your bag.'

**3** 'I can't believe we won!'

**4** 'There they are.'

**5** 'Do you want to watch a film?'

## Activity 2

| | |
|---|---|
| **A** | 6 |
| **B** | 7 |
| **C** | 3 |
| **D** | 2 |
| **E** | 4 |
| **F** | 1 |
| **G** | 5 |

## Activity 3

**1** 'I can smell trouble,' said Daniel.

**2** 'Look at that!' shouted Ned.

**3** 'Everyone looked really miserable,' said Jo.

**4** 'What are we going to do now?' cried Philip.

**5** 'We went without you,' said Lisa, 'because we didn't think you were going to turn up.'

**6** 'I don't understand,' said David. 'It doesn't make sense.'

## Activity 4

Mum, Samuel and Lucy had arrived at the theme park.

'Mum, Mum, let's go on Megaphobia first,' screamed Samuel.

'No – the pirate ship Mum,' yelled Lucy.

Mum tried to calm them by saying, 'It's all right, we'll go on both.'

'Can we buy the photo?' Lucy interrupted. 'Please, please Mum!'

'Perhaps,' she replied, 'if you stop shouting and interrupting!'

# Section 6   COMMON ERRORS

## Would/Should/Could have

**Student Book page 98**

### Activity 1

1 I **might have been** wrong to say it.

2 We **could have been** at the front if we **had been** here earlier.

3 They **should have listened** to our advice.

4 We **should have stayed** to the very end.

5 If we **had trained** more, we **would have been** in the team.

6 I **could have told** you the result before it started.

7 You **could not have been reading** the right books.

8 I *could have* been there and I *should have* been there.

## Your/You're

**Student Book page 99**

### Activity 2

1 **Your** report seems to have improved.

2 They're certain **you're** the best person for the job.

3 We're going to have to see if **you're** up to the challenge.

4 **You're** going to have to give up **your** position in the queue.

## Who's/Whose

**Student Book page 100**

### Activity 3

1 **Who's** there?

2 **Whose** is this coat?

3 I had to decide **whose** advice to follow.

4 **Who's** eaten all the rice pudding?

5 **Whose** sister did you say you saw?

## There/Their/They're

**Student Book page 101**

### Activity 4

1 **They're** going to miss **their** train.

2 **There** was early morning mist on the lake.

3 On **their** team **there** were three newcomers.

4 When they've left, **they're** going to be difficult to replace.

5 **They're** definitely going to have to get **their** act together if **they're** going to get **there** that early.

## Too/To

**Student Book page 102**

### Activity 5

1 The cyclists rode **too** fast for their own safety.

2 I have **to** tell you that sounds just **too** good **to** be true.

3 There was **too** little evidence **to** make a trial possible.

4 I'm planning **to** go **to** the cinema tonight.

5 **To** reach their goal, they had **to** face up **to** their inner fears and doubts.

## Where/Were/We're

**Student Book page 103**

### Activity 6

1 Could you please let me know when **we're** close to **where** we need to get off the bus?

2 **Where were** you when we needed you?

3 **We're** on our way – I have no idea **where**!

4 **Were** you planning to leave early to get to the place **we're** going to?

**5**   If you **were** right, **we're** nearly **where** we need to get to.

# You and me/You and I

**Student Book page 104**

## Activity 7

**1**   I told **her**. *1*

**2**   <u>To</u> **me**, it seems cold in here. *2*

**3**   Daniel asked **him**. *1*

**4**   I closed the door <u>after</u> **me**. *2*

**5**   I heard the news <u>through</u> **them**. *2*

**6**   She went to the film <u>with</u> James and **me**. *2*

**7**   Rachel and **I** were playing tennis. *1*
(**Tip:** The subject can be more than one word.)

**Note:** Prepositions that result in the use of the objective form of the pronoun are underlined.

# Section 7  APPLYING YOUR LEARNING

## Reading task

### Student Book pages 106–107

**Note:** These are sample answers. Students may well come up with valid alternatives and reasoning for some questions.

1 Both the words help to introduce the main surprise of the newspaper article – there was no one in the chairs and there was no one on board.

2 a The pronoun *they* refers to the crew.

b The newspaper article is not about anyone the reader is likely to have heard of. The important point for the reader is that the boat is empty – not the names of the crew members.

3 The verb *mystified* effectively suggests the rescue teams could not understand or explain the situation. It also links to the noun *mystery*, as in 'Mystery of *Mary Celeste* yacht' in the headline.

4 *Sunday:* proper noun for a day of the week.

*Airlie Beach:* proper noun for a particular place.

*North Queensland:* proper noun for a particular place.

*Australian:* adjective based on proper noun.

*Army Black Hawk:* proper noun for a particular name of a helicopter.

5 The journalist wants to make everything sound straightforward, simple and normal before revealing the surprise.

6 Everything about the boat seemed normal, with no sign of disturbance. *But there was no crew.* as a separate sentence has more drama and impact, suggesting the shock after the superficial normality.

7 <u>Because</u> the patrol could not make radio contact with the catamaran or see anybody aboard, a rescue helicopter was sent out on Thursday and a crewman winched down.

8 The *connective* <u>Because</u> gives a reason why the rescue helicopter was sent out, neatly explaining cause and effect to the reader in a single sentence.

9 The colon is used to introduce a quotation.

10 The quotation marks are used to indicate to the reader that the boat found was **not** called *Mary Celeste*, but that there is something about the situation that might remind a reader of the famous *Mary Celeste* yacht case.

11 The adverb *eventually* suggests a long delay before the rescue officer appears – as if he has been searching and searching for signs of life and could not believe there was no one on board.

12 No explanations seem *likely to be true*. The whole situation is full of contradictions, and it seems extremely difficult to find any logical explanation or imagine a series of events that would have led to the yacht being abandoned with no sign of disturbance and no sign of a storm.

# Part B Additional activities

## Section 1  WORDS AND PHRASES

## Prefixes, stems and suffixes

### Suffixes: Word class

#### Learning objectives

- To understand how particular suffixes form word classes.
- To understand how particular prefixes have specific meanings.
- To improve spelling by understanding regular patterns in the formation of words.

#### Activity 1 (Answers page 55)

Change the word class of each of the following words by:

- using the suffix *-able, -ly* or *-ness*
- writing three lists – each list should have words with just one suffix
- labelling each list with the previous word class, the new word class, and the chosen suffix.

| | | | | | |
|---|---|---|---|---|---|
| accept | achieve | agree | amazing | believe | bold |
| careful | change | direct | extreme | fair | faithful |
| happy | immediate | inquisitive | laugh | lively | main |
| nervous | ominous | physical | polite | reason | rely |
| remark | successful | tired | unusual | value | whole |

| Word class A:<br>Word class B:<br>Suffix = *-able* | Word class B:<br>Word class C:<br>Suffix = *-ly* | Word class B:<br>Word class D:<br>Suffix = *-ness* |
|---|---|---|
| | | |
| | | |
| | | |
| | | |

-----------------------------------------------------------------------------------------------------✂

## Prefixes: Changing the meaning

#### Activity 2 (Answers page 55)

1   Change the meaning of each of the following words by using the prefix *inter-, mis-* or *pre-*.

2   Write three lists – each list should have words with just one prefix.

3   Give a single definition for each prefix which matches each word in your list.

| | | | | | | |
|---|---|---|---|---|---|---|
| behave | cast | city | connect | face | fix | fortune |
| heat | historic | inform | kick | lead | link | national |
| net | print | set | state | view | war | |

# Nouns: Introduction to nouns

## Learning objectives

- To become more confident in recognising nouns.
- To become confident in using a range of nouns.
- To use nouns for a range of purposes.

## Activity 1

**1** Write three or more sentences taken from a commentary on a football or other match. You will probably find it easier to make the commentary up!

**2** Underline each noun you use.

Aim to include:

- a person/people: e.g. player, goalkeeper, named player
- a thing: e.g. football (the ball), sun/rain, etc., name of team
- a place: e.g. field, name of stadium
- an activity: e.g. football (the game)
- a state: e.g. excitement, boredom.

# Nouns: Common nouns

## Learning objectives

- To become more confident in recognising nouns.
- To select nouns precisely for a given purpose.
- To explore how nouns are different from other word classes.

## Activity 2 (Answers page 56)

### Working with a partner

**1** Choose a topic/hobby, without telling your partner what you have chosen.

**2** Write down a list of nouns closely connected with this topic, one at a time, letting your partner see your choices clearly, until your partner guesses precisely what the topic is. Do not say the words aloud.

The aim of the person guessing should be to come to a decision as soon as possible.

**3** Record the number of nouns taken for each topic.

**4** Is there a reason why some topics took more words than others to guess?

**5** Could you use any other word class for this activity? Why?

# Nouns: Plurals of count nouns

## Learning objectives

- To recognise and use suffixes for plurals.
- To recognise common patterns in the formation of nouns.
- To spell plural nouns accurately and independently.

## Activity 3 (Answers page 56)

Plurals in English usually end with the suffix -s or -es. It is very helpful if you know that there are a few basic patterns.

**1**  Match up the seven 'rules' for forming plurals with the examples in the table below.

**2**  Add any extra words you can think of to match each 'rule' (except 1a).

**3**  Note down any exceptions you find.

**Reminder:** The main **vowels** in English are a, e, i, o and u. The other letters of the alphabet are **consonants**.

| Type | Singular | Plural | Rule | Suffix |
|------|----------|--------|------|--------|
| 1a | book<br>dream<br>house<br>writer | books<br>dreams<br>houses<br>writers | | **-s** |
| 1b | belief<br>chief<br>proof<br>roof<br>knife<br>life<br>wife | beliefs<br>chiefs<br>proofs<br>roofs<br>knives<br>lives<br>wives | | |
| 1c | kilo<br>photo<br>radio<br>video<br>zero | kilos<br>photos<br>radios<br>videos<br>zeros | | |
| 2a | baby<br>lady<br>story<br>worry | babies<br>ladies<br>stories<br>worries | | **-es** |
| 2b | calf<br>half<br>leaf<br>loaf<br>thief | calves<br>halves<br>leaves<br>loaves<br>thieves | | |
| 2c | hero<br>mosquito<br>potato<br>tomato | heroes<br>mosquitoes<br>potatoes<br>tomatoes | | |
| 2d | branch<br>brush<br>bus<br>guess<br>hoax<br>quiz | branches<br>brushes<br>buses<br>guesses<br>hoaxes<br>quizzes | | |

### Rules

**1**  For most nouns, just add -s.

**2**  For nouns ending in a consonant + y, change the y to i before adding -es.

**3**  For nouns ending in ch, sh, s, ss, x, z just add -es.

**4**  For some nouns ending in f, change the f to v before adding -es.

**5**  For some nouns ending in f, just add -s. For nouns ending in fe, change the f to v before adding -s.

**6**  For some nouns ending in o, especially shortened nouns, just add -s.

**7**  For some nouns ending in o, just add -es.

Note: *quiz* to *quizzes* gains an extra z.

# Pronouns: How to use pronouns

## Learning objectives

- To increase the range of noun phrases you can use.

- To increase your understanding of how noun phrases can be built up.

- To increase your confidence in recognising noun phrases by replacing each one with a pronoun.

## Activity (Answers page 57)

**1**   Create at least three sentences using words from the four columns in the table below. You can choose more than one adjective from the third column in a single sentence. You can add words *before* or *after* the given words to complete the sentence.

**2**   Underline the noun phrase you create in each case. Check if you can replace it with a pronoun.

| | | | |
|---|---|---|---|
| a | two | adventure | in China |
| the | best | football | in the shop |
| some | exciting | lap-top | on television |
| all | expensive | mountain | which I borrowed |
| this | | running | with extra features |
| those | | bicycle(s) | |
| his | | computer(s) | |
| her | | games | |
| their | | holiday(s) | |
| David's | | shoes(s) | |
| Ann's | | | |

Note: a **noun phrase** can include adjectives and prepositions and verbs. They do not always include a noun, but if not they will just consist of a single pronoun.

# Adjectives: Selecting adjectives for impact

## Learning objectives

- To increase your confidence in recognising adjectives.
- To increase your understanding of how adjectives can be used in different ways.
- To establish a variety of ways of using adjectives in your own writing.

## Activity 1 (Answers page 57)

**1**   Decide which of the adjectives below fits best in each of the gaps.

**2**   As you write down each adjective, draw an arrow to the right if the noun it refers to comes later in the sentence.

**3**   As you write down each adjective, draw an arrow to the left if the noun it refers to comes earlier in the sentence.

e.g. *tall* → man ← *taller*

He was a _____ man and every year he looked a little _____. He had

_____ _____ hair which looked OK from a long way away – only when you got closer you

could see the _____ _____ surface of his skull. His trousers, even on the _____

summer day, were _____ and _____, as were his glasses. These were

_____ with _____ _____ frames and _____ _____ sorts of glass.

| bright | different | enormous | black | heavy | hottest |
|--------|-----------|----------|-------|-------|---------|
| | pink | tall   taller | silver | speckled | |
| | | thick   two   wiry | | | |

**Now:**

**4**   Find an adjective that comes before the noun it describes.

**5**   Find an adjective that comes after the noun it describes.

**6**   Choose what you think is the most effective adjective here, and be ready to justify your choice.

# Adjectives: Comparatives and superlatives

## Learning objectives

- To recognise and use common patterns for forming comparatives and superlatives.
- To know how to form common irregular comparatives and superlatives.
- To increase your choices in using adjectives, establishing how most adjectives can be used in six different ways.

## Activity 2 (Answers page 57)

**Comparatives** are formed by either adding the suffix -er (e.g. *kind to kinder*) or inserting *more* before the adjective (e.g. *more* interesting).

**Superlatives** are formed by either adding the suffix -est (e.g. *kind to kindest*) or inserting *most* before the adjective (e.g. *most* interesting).

**1**   Fill in the gaps in the table below.

| Original adjective | Comparative | Superlative |
|---|---|---|
| bad | | |
| few | | |
| good | | |
| little | | |
| many/much | | |

**2**   Now complete the table below, filling in the missing panels.

| Lowest degree | Lower degree | Same degree | Higher degree (comparative) | Highest degree (superlative) |
|---|---|---|---|---|
| least attractive | less attractive | as attractive as | more attractive | most attractive |
| least beautiful | | | | |
| | | | | cheapest |
| | | | | most effective |
| | | | more exciting | |
| | less successful | | | |
| least tasty | | | | |

# Verbs: The different ways we can use a verb

## Learning objectives

- To understand how to use the infinitive and imperative of a verb.
- To understand how to build verb phrases, using auxiliary verbs.
- To recognise how many choices you have in varying meaning with *each* verb you use.

## Activity 1 (Answers page 58)

How many ways do you think you can use a single verb such as *speak*? For example:

- the infinitive: I need *to speak* to you in private.
- the imperative: *Speak up!*

These are just two of the ways you can use *speak*. Write down your estimate for the total number of ways you can use the verb *speak*.

### Step 1: Not using auxiliary verbs

**1**    Write down as many forms of the verb *to speak* as you can think of, e.g., *I speak*.

**2**    Think of present tense and past tense, but do not use any verbs apart from *to speak*.

**3**    You can count each person (*I, you,* etc.) as a different form of the verb.

### Note for Step 1

- The only verb you can use is *to speak*.
- You can use present and past tense.
- Count *I/you* (singular)*/he/she/we/you* (plural)*/they* examples separately.

### Step 2: Using auxiliary verbs

If you were restricted to just using one verb on its own, your talking and writing would be very limited. There are three verbs that can be both an **auxiliary** verb and a **main** verb: *to be, to do* and *to have*. We saw that just using the verb *to speak* on its own was very limiting.

**4**    Now see what you can add to your list of versions of *to speak* by including the auxiliary verb *to be* in any of its forms.

**5**    Write down at least five examples, e.g. *I am speaking*.

### Note for Step 2

The only verbs you can use are *to be* and *to speak*.

### Step 3

**6**    Now see what you can add by including the auxiliary verb *to have* in any of its forms.

**7**    Write down at least five examples, e.g. *I have spoken*.

### Note for Step 3

The only verbs you can use are *to have* and *to speak*.

See page 32 for Steps 4–7 of this activity.

## Activity 1 continued

### Step 4

**8**    Now see what you can add by including the auxiliary verb *to do* in any of its forms.

**9**    Write down at least five examples, e.g. *I do speak clearly.*

### Note for Step 4

The only verbs you can use are *to do* and *to speak*.

### Step 5

Apart from the auxiliary verbs *to be, to have* and *to do*, there are also auxiliary verbs which **cannot** be main verbs. (One way to check is by trying to use the verb in the infinitive: you can use *to be, to have* and *to do*, but not *to could, to must* or *to should*.)

**10**    Now see what you can add by including any of the following auxiliary verbs:

> *can    could    may    might    must    ought to    shall    should    will*

**11**    Write down at least five examples, e.g. *I could speak.*

### Note for Step 5

The only verbs you can use are the nine auxiliary verbs listed above and *to speak*.

### Step 6

**12**    Finally, see what choices you have if you combine any of the auxiliary verbs you have used so far.

**13**    Decide if the auxiliary verbs have to be in any particular order.

### Step 7

**14**    Count how many verb phrases you have created just based on the verb *to speak*. Compare your present estimate of how many versions there could be of the verb *to speak* (+ auxiliary verbs) with your original estimate.

  You may find you have many more than you predicted at the beginning! This just shows how flexible you can be in making your meaning clear with just one main verb.

**15**    In a pair, write down what choices you have when using a verb.

# Verbs: Effective use of verbs

## Learning objectives

- To increase the range and variety of verbs you choose.
- To have practice in choosing just the right verb for a particular context.
- To encourage the use of dynamic verbs when appropriate.

## Activity 2 (Answers page 59)

Twenty verbs have been removed from the passage below, which was written by a student.

**1**    From the list, decide which is the most appropriate verb for each gap and write it in.

**2**    Which choice of verb do you think is most effective and why?

**3**    Which choice of verb do you think is least effective and why?

**4**    Suggest one specific way in which this writing could be improved by using a different verb, or by using a verb in a different way.

Chips _____ and _____ as they were _____ out of the fryer, oil

_____ off them like a waterfall. Customers _____ and _____ in a

constant cycle, _____ and _____ in the queue. Fish _____,

newspaper _____, gravy _____ and fat _____. Bubbles

_____ for air as they _____ from under the chips. The potato machine

_____ as it _____ out another batch. The till _____ as it was

_____ shut, _____ as it _____ more money.

| | | | | | |
|---|---|---|---|---|---|
| bubbled | chimed | crackled | dragged | draining | dripped |
| entered | gargled | gasped | gulping | hissed | jostling |
| left | pushing | rose | rustled | slammed | sloshed |
| | | spat | swallowed | | |

# Verbs: Verb forms

## Learning objectives

- To understand the different forms a verb can take.
- To understand what form to use with an auxiliary verb.
- To avoid making mistakes in verbs in standard English.

## Activity 3 (Answers page 60)

Verbs have a variety of different forms. In most cases, the *past form* and the *-ed participle* are the same. Many of the errors students make are with verbs in which these two forms are different.

You will need to refer to this table to complete the activity.

| base | present | past | *-ing* participle | *-ed* participle |
|------|---------|------|-------------------|------------------|
| **be** | am, is, are | was, were | being | been |
| **do** | do, does | did | doing | done |
| **go** | go, goes | went | going | gone |
| **have** | have, has | had | having | had |
| **kick** | kick, kicks | kicked | kicking | kicked |
| **sit** | sit, sits | sat | sitting | sat |
| **speak** | speak, speaks | spoke | speaking | spoken |
| **write** | write, writes | wrote | writing | written |

Below are some examples of standard and non-standard use of these verbs.

**1**   Place a tick in the first blank column if there is an auxiliary verb (*be, have, do*) **before** the main verb. Otherwise place a cross.

**2**   Place a tick in the second blank column if the main verb is in the *participle* form. (Check against the table above.) Otherwise place a cross.

**3**   Which combinations are allowed in standard English?

| | Sentence example | Auxiliary verb before main verb? | Participle form? | Standard English? |
|---|------------------|----------------------------------|------------------|-------------------|
| **1** | He had written it himself. | | | |
| **2** | She did the crossword before breakfast. | | | |
| **3** | The newspaper is wrote in a different way. | | | |
| **4** | She done her homework quickly. | | | |
| **5** | They had already gone out. | | | |

# Adverbs: Using adverbs correctly

## Learning objectives

- To understand when to use adverbs rather than adjectives.
- To understand how to use adverbs in standard English.
- To extend choices in where to place the adverb in a sentence.

## Activity 1 (Answers page 60)

There are problems with the use of adverbs in the following three examples. Identify one problem in each case, and give a one-sentence piece of advice to the writer in each case.

**1** You've got to do it quick.

**2** Squinting up ahead he could see nothing but white, and his hope seeped away, but he drove himself on, walking blind through the snow.

**3** Laughing voices happily filled the air of the candle-lit room as she cheerfully walked towards the round table in the centre of the room to carefully take the orders from the party of twelve already seated and merrily drinking.

--------------------------------------------------------------------------------------- ✀

# Adverbs: Varying your use of adverbs

## Learning objectives

- To recognise how adverbs are used before and after the words they modify.
- To recognise how adverbs modify adjectives and verbs.
- To extend the range of ways you use adverbs in your own writing.

## Activity 2 (Answers page 60)

**1** Study the use of adverbs in the following extract, which is about someone taking the controls of a plane for the first time.

**2** Write down the adverbs and any words they modify/link to.

**3** Decide whether the adverb comes **before** or **after** the word it is modifying, and whether this is a **verb** or an **adjective**. Also decide if any are sentence connectors.

**4** Write a set of suggestions about how to vary the way you use adverbs.

Paint had peeled off large stretches of the fuselage, leaving suspiciously rusty patches.
'Would you like to try take-off?'
Jackson casually waved at the control stick in front of me.
I stared at him in disbelief. 'You must be mad! I've never even been in a cockpit before.'
'Honestly, there's nothing to it. Besides, I'll be following you on my controls.'
I did exactly as I was told. The plane rocked and bounced down the airstrip, and I silently urged the speed indicator to rise before we reached the trees at the far end. Finally, the needle crept up to the mark and I brought the column back, fascinated as my effortless actions lifted us off the ground. The plane rocked slightly, but then eased into a smooth climb, comfortably missing the perimeter trees.

From *The Mind Game* by Hector MacDonald

# Adverbs: Adverbials

## Learning objectives

- To recognise adverbials.
- To identify different types of adverbials.
- To increase your choices in writing by gaining confidence in using adverbials.

## Activity 3 (Answers page 60)

Read the following two sentences.

- We got home *early*.
- We got home *at six in the morning*.

In the first sentence, *early* is an adverb. But *at six in the morning* in the second sentence gives you similar information – **when** they got home. *at six in the morning* is an example of what is called an **adverbial**. A single adverb like *early* can also be referred to as an adverbial.

Read the following list and copy the adverbials into the table below according to the kind of question they answer. Find the heading that fits most closely in each case. There are two adverbials in each section; the first one has been completed for you.

**1**  *At the weekend,* I'm going out with my friends.

**2**  *Because of the rain* the match was cancelled.

**3**  *Every other Saturday* we have a training session.

**4**  *For a fortnight* we didn't see them at all.

**5**  I entered the competition *for fun*.

**6**  It was quicker to travel *by train*.

**7**  She lives *in Paris*.

**8**  The mobile library comes *each week*.

**9**  The pool is *about 10 metres long*.

**10**  The surfboard was finished *by hand*.

**11**  They finally got back *after midnight*.

**12**  They were staying in tents *with a group of friends*.

**13**  This bus route takes you straight *to the stadium*.

**14**  We decided to go *on our own*.

| Where? | |
| --- | --- |
| When? | At the weekend. |
| How long? | |
| How often? | |
| How? | |
| Why? | |
| With whom? | |

Grammar Matters Too Teacher Resource File © Pearson Education Ltd

# Prepositions: Time and movement

## Learning objectives

- To recognise prepositions.
- To understand how prepositions can be used in different ways.
- To gain confidence in using a variety of prepositions in your own writing.

## Activity 1

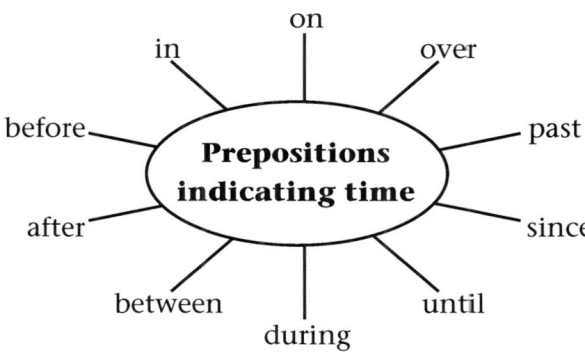

Suppose you arrive home one evening later than expected, or a teacher is asking why you were not in the expected place at the expected time. You have to explain what you were doing during this time.

**1**  Write five sentences using at least five prepositions of time. Use a noun after your preposition.

**2**  Underline each preposition you use.

**3**  Try not to use the same preposition more than once, e.g. <u>After</u> breakfast and <u>before</u> first lesson I …

**Warning:** Some of these words can be used in other ways. Make sure you only underline prepositions of time.

- *Since* (= because) it was time for first lesson … ✗
- I had been there *since* 10 o'clock. ✓

## Activity 2

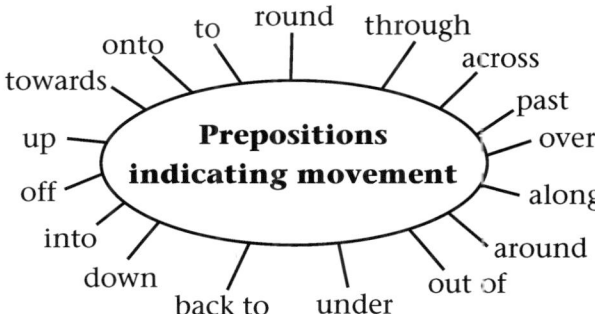

**1**  Write five sentences describing a sport involving plenty of movement, such as football, basketball or tennis.

**2**  Include at least one of the prepositions from the list above in each sentence. Only use each preposition once.

**3**  Underline each preposition (where to?) that you use, e.g. The forward went <u>through</u> the gap between two defenders and passed the ball <u>along</u> the ground halfway <u>across</u> the pitch.

---

# Section 2 SENTENCES

# What is a sentence?

## Learning objectives

- To understand how to form sentences in different ways.
- To understand the terms subject, object, complement and adverbial.
- To increase the range of sentence patterns you can choose to use in your own writing.

### Activity 1 Subject + Verb (SV)

**1** Write at least five sentences using one noun and one verb from the table below.

**2** Do not use the same noun or verb twice.

| Noun/pronoun (subject of sentence) | Verb |
|---|---|
| A door | emptied |
| I | escaped |
| London | grew |
| The car | left |
| The horse | opened |
| The room | ran |
| The woman | reversed |

### Activity 2 Subject + Verb + Object (SVO)

**1** Write at least five sentences using one item from each column from the table below.

**2** Do not use the same subject or verb twice.

| Subject | Verb | Noun/pronoun (object of sentence) |
|---|---|---|
| Her brother | ate | a goal |
| I | chose | her e-mails |
| Sarah | cooked | its food |
| The boy | left | our meal |
| The cat | opened | that holiday |
| The chef | prepared | the ingredients |
| The teacher | scored | the room |

### Activity 3 Subject + Verb + Complement (SVC)

**1** Write at least five sentences using one item from each column from the table below.

**2** Do not use the same words twice.

| Subject | Verb | Complement |
|---|---|---|
| Graham | ended up | anxious |
| My house | felt | delicious |
| Our teacher | is | the winners |
| The day | is | Mrs Jones |
| The food | tasted | hot |
| The room | turned out | No. 7 |
| Their team | was | fine |

### Activity 4 Subject + Verb + Adverbial (SVA)

**1** Write at least five sentences using one item from each column from the table below.

**2** Do not use the same words twice.

| Subject | Verb | Adverbial |
|---|---|---|
| His brother | arrived | by a bee (how?) |
| I | cycled | for a week (when – how long?) |
| My aunt | entered | from home (where from?) |
| She | spoke | on Sunday (when?) |
| The umpire | stayed | silently (how?) |
| They | walked | to school (where to?) |
| We | was stung | without notes (how?) |

Grammar Matters Too Teacher Resource File © Pearson Education Ltd

# Simple sentences

## Learning objectives

- To write clear instructions using simple sentences.
- To understand how to form simple sentences.
- To increase the range of sentence patterns you can use with confidence.

## Activity

Making a paper aeroplane – writing instructions in simple sentences.

For this activity you will need two A4 sheets of paper and something to make notes on.

**1**  Take one of the sheets of paper and make a paper aeroplane.

**2**  Using simple sentences only, write instructions for somebody else on how to make another paper aeroplane of the same shape and design as the one you have just made.

**3**  Follow your instructions carefully, doing only what you have written down. Has the second paper aeroplane turned out the same? Did you find your instructions easy? Was there anything you had left out?

**4**  Make a few brief notes on how your instructions worked and how they might have been improved.

# Checking agreement

## Learning objectives

- To identify the subject of a sentence.
- To understand different ways of forming a subject.
- To vary your choices in using a subject in your own writing.

## Activity (Answers page 61)

Make a list of the subjects in the following book review of *Chasing Redbird* by Sharon Creech. Look for **nouns**, **pronouns** or **noun phrases**.

> It's easy to identify with Zinny in this warm and funny story about the confusion of growing up and the need to find a true sense of yourself. Her rumbustious family, with its three boys and four girls, lives in a rambling farm with their aunt and uncle next door. For Zinny, Uncle Nate's and Aunt Jessie's house has always been a sanctuary where she can talk and be heard, something she finds hard in her own home. But when her beloved Auntie Jessie dies unexpectedly, Zinny finds it hard to get her bearings. Her thoughts are like tangled spaghetti and she cannot put them back in order.

# Object, Complement and Adverbial

## Learning objectives

- To identify the object or complement in a sentence.
- To understand different ways of forming an object, complement or adverbial.
- To vary your choices in using an object or complement in your own writing.

## Activity 1 (Answers page 61)

Read through the list below. It contains the instructions for putting up a flat-packed home-assembly bookcase, but the instructions have been jumbled up. Read through the instructions carefully, then write them out and number them in the correct order. Underline the objects in each instruction. For example:

1  Unwrap all the components and lay them out all over the floor.

> - Fit the shelves.
> - Count all the pieces and check them.
> - Fix the second upright to the top of the bookcase.
> - Fit the screws provided into the ready-drilled holes.
> - Fix the shelf supports into the ready-drilled holes in the second upright at the same intervals as the first.
> - Stand the bookcase in the desired location.
> - Take one of the longest planks (uprights) and fix the top plank to it.
> - Line up the ready-drilled screw-holes and use the screws provided.
> - Unwrap all the components and lay them out all over the floor.

## Activity 2

Rewrite this short paragraph, making it more interesting. Include some adverbials explaining where, when, how and to what extent things happened. For example, 'Sam got off the bus in the town centre at eight thirty on Saturday morning ...'

> Sam got off the bus. She came down the road. She came to a shop. She went in. She bought an ice cream. She came outside. She stood by the telephone box. She made a phone call. She sat down on the bench. She waited. A bus stopped. Her friend leapt off. They made their way to the ice rink. They waited for her friends.

# Section 3   BUILDING   SENTENCES

## Building simple sentences

### Learning objectives

- To understand how to form a simple sentence.
- To understand the problems if a writer uses a series of simple sentences.
- To have a range of strategies for varying sentence patterns in your writing.

### Activity (Answers page 62)

Assess the piece of writing opposite in pairs, noting down three precise things you think are good about it, and one clear piece of advice for improvement.

I felt sick with fear. I looked around. I saw nobody. I heard nothing. I was alone. I felt terrified. I ran for the exit. I crashed into some chairs. I hurt my knee. I knew I had to get out. I might be trapped for ever. I ignored the pain. I forced my way through the door. I saw a policeman. I ran to him. I was screaming. I was trembling. I grabbed his arm. He must have been surprised by my appearance and behaviour. He was calm and patient.

## Clauses

### Learning objectives

- To recognise different types of clause.
- To understand how sentences are built from clauses.
- To increase the range of sentence patterns you can choose to use in your own writing.

### Activity

Almost all sentences are built up from these seven types of *clause*:

| | | |
|---|---|---|
| **1** | S + V | James spoke. |
| **2** | S + V + O | James played the piano. |
| **3** | S + V + C | James was nervous. |
| **4** | S + V + A | James arrived on Monday. |
| **5** | S + V + O + O | James gave us his keys. |
| **6** | S + V + O + C | James found the door open. |
| **7** | S + V + O + A | James placed his winnings on the table. |

**Note**

- S, the subject and O, the object, will be in the form of a noun phrase.
- V will be in the form of a verb phrase.
- A will be in the form of an adverbial.
- C is the complement.

The **phrase** is the building block of the **clause**.

The **clause** is the basic building block of a **sentence**, just as the **morpheme** is the basic building block of a **word**.

1   Write seven sentences, one of each type of clause.

2   You can model them very closely on the examples above if you wish, but make sure you change most of the words.

# Compound sentences

## Learning objectives

- To understand how to form compound sentences.

- To understand how to vary the pattern of sentences in your writing.

- To improve a piece of writing by carefully choosing when to use simple sentences and when to use compound sentences.

## Activity (Answers page 62)

If you join two or more **simple sentences** with *and*, *but* or *or*, you form a compound sentence.

Now rewrite the passage opposite in your pairs/threes. The rules are:

- you can only add the connectives *and*, *but* or *or*

- you can make changes to punctuation

- no other changes are allowed.

Assess this new piece of writing, noting down three precise things you think are good about it, and one clear piece of advice for improvement. As you hear other groups read their versions, decide which you think is the most effective and why.

> I felt sick with fear. I looked around. I saw nobody. I heard nothing. I was alone. I felt terrified. I ran for the exit. I crashed into some chairs. I hurt my knee. I knew I had to get out. I might be trapped for ever. I ignored the pain. I forced my way through the door. I saw a policeman. I ran to him. I was screaming. I was trembling. I grabbed his arm. He must have been surprised by my appearance and behaviour. He was calm and patient.

# Connectives

## Learning objectives

- To understand how to choose connectives to form complex sentences.

- To understand how to vary the pattern of sentences by placing the connective in different places.

- To understand how you can form sentences with the precise meaning and impact you require.

## Activity (Answers page 62)

If you have a range of ways of writing the same idea, you are in a much better position to convey to your audience exactly what you want. In this activity, you will experiment with changing sentences around and exploring the effect of each change.

For example, look at these two separate sentences:
*The team had lost heavily. The coach said he would resign.*

Many alternatives are possible, such as:
*Because the team had lost heavily, the coach said he would resign.*
*The coach said he would resign as the team had lost heavily.*

**1**  Rewrite each of the following pairs of sentences (a, b and c) as a single complex sentence. Try to find at least two ways of doing this for each pair, using connectives. You can change the order of the sentences.

**2**  In each case, decide which of your own versions sounds best.

**3**  In each case, decide which version from the rest of the class sounds best.

**a**  This event comes around once a year. I have a year to recover from it.

**b**  If you have a family then the beach scene would appeal to you. If you are single then the white-water rafting picture might appeal to you.

**c**  He was always willing to help. I was his favourite nephew.

| **Possible connectives** |
| --- |
| as    because    since    so    whereas    while |

# Complex sentences

## Learning objectives

- To understand how to form complex sentences by using certain connectives.
- To understand how to form complex sentences by using the *-ing* and *-ed* forms of verbs.
- To improve writing by carefully choosing when to use simple sentences and when to use different types of complex sentence.

## Activity (Answers page 63)

If you join two or more **simple sentences** with connectives such as *when, so* or *although*, you form a complex sentence. You can also form a complex sentence if you use the *-ing* or *-ed* forms of verbs.

**1**    Now rewrite this passage in your pairs/threes. The rules are:

- you can use any connectives, such as *when, so* or *although*
- you can delete words so long as you keep the basic structure
- you can change any verbs into their *-ing* form or *-ed* form, e.g. *Feeling sick with fear …*

> I felt sick with fear. I looked around. I saw nobody. I heard nothing. I was alone. I felt terrified. I ran for the exit. I crashed into some chairs. I hurt my knee. I knew I had to get out. I might be trapped for ever. I ignored the pain. I forced my way through the door. I saw a policeman. I ran to him. I was screaming. I was trembling. I grabbed his arm. He must have been surprised by my appearance and behaviour. He was calm and patient.

**2**    Assess this new piece of writing, noting down three precise things you think are good about it, and one clear piece of advice for improvement. As you hear other groups read their versions, decide which you think is the most effective.

**3**    Now write some advice for yourself and others in your group about using a range of sentence patterns. You should make reference to **connectives**, **simple sentences**, **compound sentences** and **complex sentences** in your advice. Write down any good advice you hear for use in your future writing – in any subject inside or outside school.

# Section 4  PARAGRAPHS AND WHOLE TEXTS

## Organising your ideas into paragraphs

### Learning objectives

- To prepare for writing about a topic by generating questions.
- To organise these questions into logical groupings.
- To organise these groupings into logical paragraphs, understanding why paragraphs are used.

### Activity (Answers page 63)

Shortly, you will be writing about a person you know well, perhaps a brother or sister or a friend, so that a reader who does not know them will gain a clear idea of what they are like. Before you start writing you need to organise your ideas into logical groups.

**1**  Write a set of questions you think a reader might like answered on the person you are describing. You could include questions on some of the following:

- achievements
- age
- appearance
- clothing for different purposes
- eye/hair colour/hair style
- favourite books/music/sport
- favourite possession
- friendship groups
- habits
- height
- hobbies
- overall character/personality
- typical footwear
- typical leisure time activities

As you hear good questions from other students, add them to your list.

**Advice:**

- Organise your questions into logical groups, e.g. everything about physical appearance together.
- Organise these logical groups into a logical order, e.g. what would it be helpful for a reader to know first? These groupings will form your paragraphs.
- Discuss with another pair of students the decisions you have taken and why you have taken them.
- Discuss your final paragraph plan for writing about a person you know well, taking into account any suggestions from other students.

**2**  Now write the full text, describing a person you know well, taking particular care over the organisation of your writing into paragraphs.

# Section 5   PUNCTUATION

## Capital letters

### Learning objectives

- To explore different reasons for using capital letters.
- To be able to explain why capital letters are used in any particular case.
- To use capital letters appropriately for a range of purposes when writing.

### Activity (Answers page 63)

Match up the following uses of capital letters to the reasons for using them:

**1**   "DON'T GO THERE!"

**2**   BIGGEST TRAVELLING FAIR IN BRITAIN

**3**   ROMEO:  He jests at scars that never felt a wound.

**4**   She ate a Bounty Bar to give herself extra energy for the match.

---

**Reasons**

**A**   Capital letters for the first letters of brand names.

**B**   Capitals for name of character speaking, in some play scripts.

**C**   Capitals for some public signs, intended to make them bolder and more visible.

**D**   Capitals to indicate that the speaker is talking loudly.

---

## Question marks

### Learning objectives

- To understand the difference between rhetorical questions and non-rhetorical questions.

### Activity (Answers page 64)

Speakers and writers sometimes use **questions** when they are not in fact asking for information, but wish to make a point strongly.  Questions which are not asking for information are called **rhetorical questions**.

Decide which of the following are **rhetorical questions**, which *do not expect a spoken answer*, and which are questions that *do expect a spoken answer*:

**1**   Are you coming out tonight?

**2**   Can *anyone* put up with that sort of behaviour?

**3**   Do you own a pair of Trailblazers yet?

**4**   Have you been selected for the team?

**5**   Wouldn't you prefer to have your home safe at night?

# Commas

## Learning objectives

- To understand a range of reasons for using commas.
- To identify the reason for using a comma in a given context.
- To increase your ability to use commas accurately for a range of specific purposes.

## Activity (Answers page 64)

The following list shows the main reasons for using commas.

**A** To divide items in a list:

*Her favourite sports are football, tennis and skating.*

(A comma before the *and* is optional.)

**B** To separate different adjectives:

*He was tall, dark and handsome.*

**C** To separate the subordinate clause from the main clause when the subordinate clause comes first:

*When I arrived home, my sister ran to welcome me.*

**D** To make clear exactly who a relative clause is referring to:

*The boys, who wanted to play the match, were disappointed when it was postponed.*

This suggests all the boys wanted to play the match.

*The boys who wanted to play the match were disappointed when it was postponed.*

This suggests some boys wanted to play the match, and only these boys were disappointed.

**E** At the beginning and end of direct speech:

*Daniel said, 'I'll join you later.'*

*'I'm glad you can spare the time,' I replied.*

**F** After an adverb at the beginning of a sentence:

*However, this was not the end of the incident.*

**G** To make five-figure and larger numbers easier to read.

*1,563,257*

**1** Write out the following sentences and insert commas where they are needed.

**2** Indicate why the comma is being used in each case by writing A, B, C, D, E, F or G above each comma you insert.

    **a** A megabyte equals 1048576 bytes.

    **b** If it doesn't rain we could go to the park.

    **c** Elaine asked 'Where are we going?'

    **d** She wore a beautiful new sparkly black dress.

    **e** Carefully he opened the door.

    **f** The drivers who knew about the floods took another route.

    **g** On holiday we visited towns in France Spain Portugal and Italy.

# Apostrophes

## Learning objectives

● To understand the use of the apostrophe of 'possession' in English.

● To help you work out exactly where to place the apostrophe of 'possession'.

● To increase your ability to use the apostrophe of 'possession' accurately every time.

## Activity 1 (Answers page 64)

Nouns can often be used in the singular or plural (friend, friends). But you can also add **'s or s'** to many nouns. This means that nouns in English usually have four forms, e.g. *friend, friends, friend's, friends'*.

If you are translating *the boy's head* into French, you need to translate *the head of the boy* (*la tête du garçon*). This is because the English language has a quick and short way of indicating *the head of the boy* (*the boy's head*), but the French language does not.

This form is often called **the possessive** (belonging to).

Decide how far **possessive** is a good term to use for these examples:

**a**    a week's holiday = holiday *for* a week

**b**    a summer's day = a day *in* summer

**c**    Charles Dickens' novels = novels *by* Charles Dickens

**d**    Friday's announcement = the announcement *on* Friday

**e**    Graham's dog = the dog *of* Graham

**f**    yesterday's news = the news *from* yesterday

## Activity 2 (Answers page 64)

The apostrophe indicates *of, for, by, from, in, on* the noun the apostrophe is attached to. For example:
The boy's head = the head *of* the boy.
The women's team = the team *of* the women.

**1**    Write out the following (a–f) in a fuller version, keeping the same meaning but avoiding using an apostrophe.

**2**    Write down the last letter of the last word of your sentence, and compare this with the position of the apostrophe. For example, a. An evening in winter. Last letter = r.

**a**    A winter's evening.

**b**    Each other's work.

**c**    Parents' evening.

**d**    Philip Pullman's trilogy.

**e**    The girls' gym.

**f**    The referee's decision.

# Apostrophes continued

You may ask:

'How can I get the apostrophe right every time?'

You need to understand *why* the apostrophe is there if you are going to get it right every time.

| Singular | *of*, *for*, *by*, *from*, *in*, *on* (the singular noun) | Plural | *of*, *for*, *by*, *from*, *in*, *on* (the plural noun) |
|---|---|---|---|
| friend | **friend's**<br>My friend's house = the house *of* my frien**d**. | friends | **friends'**<br>My friends' houses = the houses *of* my friend**s**. |
| week | **week's**<br>One week's holiday = holiday *for* one wee**k**. | weeks | **weeks'**<br>Two weeks' holiday = holiday *for* two week**s**. |
| woman | **woman's**<br>The woman's career = the career *of* the woma**n**. | women | **women's**<br>The women's team = team *for* wome**n**. |
| Dickens | **Dickens'**<br>Dickens' novels = novels *by* Dicken**s**. | Joneses | **Joneses'**<br>The Joneses' son = the son *of* the Jonese**s**. |
| child | **child's**<br>The child's decision = the decision *of/by* the chil**d**. | children | **children's**<br>The children's games = the games *of/for* the childre**n**. |
| other | **other's**<br>each other's ideas = the ideas *of/from* each othe**r**. | others | **others'**<br>all the others' ideas = the ideas *of/from* all the other**s**. |
| | **Note that the singular can be 's or, when the noun ends in -s, s' e.g. James' aunt** | | **Note that the plural can be 's or s'** |

The only safe way to check if your apostrophe is in the right place is to turn the sentence the other way round and see what the last letter is (as above, in **bold**).

Suppose you have written:

*They embarrassed me on Parent's Evening.*

When you check, you say in your head: *They embarrassed me on the Evening for Parent. ...* **stopping before the apostrophe**. You will know this is wrong, and can change it to:

*They embarrassed me on Parents' Evening.*

When you check your correction, you say in your head: *They embarrassed me on the evening for Parents.* And know it is right.

**Note:** Do not use apostrophes to indicate plurals.

## Activity 3 (Answers page 65)

These are examples from students' writing that include mistakes. Write out the part that is wrong, and write a note to the student explaining:

● what they need to change

● why they need to change it

● if possible, a strategy for avoiding making this mistake again.

    **a**    Some OAP's walk through the doors.

    **b**    Sweaty, hot and bothered employee's try to do their best in pleasing customers.

# Colons

## Learning objectives

- To understand a range of reasons for using colons.
- To identify the reason for using a colon in a given context.
- To increase your ability to use colons accurately for a range of specific purposes.

## Activity (Answers page 65)

The following list shows the main reasons for using colons.

**A** To introduce a list of items:

*To make this fruit smoothie you will need: a banana, an apple, a mango and some natural yoghurt.*

**B** To separate two clauses in a sentence, when the second clause gives more information about the first:

*Compasses are really useful: they help you to find your way.*

**C** To introduce a quotation, saying or rule:

*Remember what Grandma always says: an apple a day keeps the doctor away.*

**1** Write out the following sentences (a–d) and insert colons where they are needed, changing other punctuation as necessary.

   **a** She decided not to argue the holiday was already booked.

   **b** To make scrambled eggs you need milk, butter and eggs.

   **c** As the train manager said driving the train is only half the story.

**2** Indicate why the colon is being used in each case by writing A, B or C above each colon you insert.

# Semi-colons

## Learning objectives

- To understand a range of reasons for using semi-colons.
- To identify the reason for using a semi-colon in a given context.
- To increase your ability to use semi-colons accurately for a range of specific purposes.

## Activity (Answers page 65)

The following list shows the main reasons for using semi-colons.

**A**  To separate longer items in a list:

*I have visited: Paris, the capital of France; Cardiff, the capital of Wales; and Edinburgh, the capital of Scotland.*

**B**  To divide up long sentences:

*It wasn't just the swerve; it wasn't just the speed; each bounce zigzagged across the pitch as if the ball had a life of its own!*

**C**  To introduce a contrast:

*Some people like to go outside in the rain; others prefer to stay indoors.*

**Note:** A semi-colon is not followed by a capital letter (unless, of course, the word following the semi-colon is a proper noun). In the case of C, the semi-colon could be replaced by a connective such as *but* or *while*.

**1**   Write out the following sentences (a–c) and insert semi-colons where they are needed, changing other punctuation as necessary.

    **a**   I like pasta she likes curry.

    **b**   She loves ballet and tap dancing running and cycling and all sorts of reading.

    **c**   The bus was late I got to school late the day had started badly.

**2**   Indicate why the semi-colon is being used in each case by writing A, B or C above each semi-colon you insert.

# Speech marks/inverted commas

## Learning objectives

- To create rules for the correct use of punctuation of speech by studying a correct version.
- To identify the reason for using a particular punctuation mark in a given context.
- To increase your ability to use punctuation and paragraphing accurately when including direct speech in your writing.

## Activity (Answers page 65)

1   Working in groups create a list of instructions for speech punctuation by comparing Versions 1 and 2 of the text below. Try to include all the rules you would need in order to change Version 1 to Version 2. Write one clear and precise instruction for each numbered arrow.

2   Aim to make your instructions clear, direct and easy to follow. For instruction 2, try to make your instruction fit any possible punctuation mark.

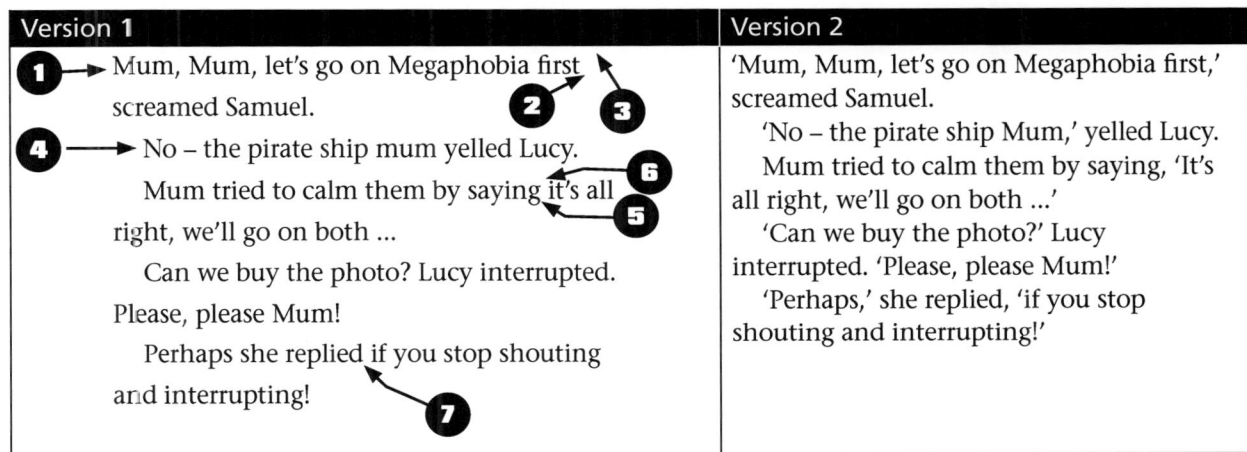

| Version 1 | Version 2 |
|---|---|
| Mum, Mum, let's go on Megaphobia first screamed Samuel.<br><br>No – the pirate ship mum yelled Lucy.<br>Mum tried to calm them by saying it's all right, we'll go on both ...<br>Can we buy the photo? Lucy interrupted. Please, please Mum!<br>Perhaps she replied if you stop shouting and interrupting! | 'Mum, Mum, let's go on Megaphobia first,' screamed Samuel.<br>　'No – the pirate ship Mum,' yelled Lucy.<br>　Mum tried to calm them by saying, 'It's all right, we'll go on both ...'<br>　'Can we buy the photo?' Lucy interrupted. 'Please, please Mum!'<br>　'Perhaps,' she replied, 'if you stop shouting and interrupting!' |

3   As you listen to each instruction suggested by other groups, make any changes you think would improve your set of instructions.

# Section 6 COMMON ERRORS

## Learning objectives

- To understand the possible meanings of *who's*.
- To understand when to use *whose* appropriately.
- To avoid confusing *who's* and *whose*.

# Who's/Whose

## Activity (Answers page 66)

Here are some examples of how to use *whose* appropriately.

- Whose bike were you riding yesterday?
- We do not know whose these are.
- I would like to thank my mentor, without whose help I could not have achieved so much.

*who's* sounds the same, but is short for *who is* or *who has*.

In the following questions, identify which is short for *who is* and which is short for *who has*.

**1** Who's been sleeping in my bed?   **3** Who's going to take you home?

**2** Who's in the kitchen?   **4** Who's eaten the last chocolate?

If you think you may make mistakes with this spelling, use the following strategy.

*Whenever you use* **who's**, *say to yourself* **who is** *or* **who has.**

When proofreading: 'Who's on the team list?' I asked. Say to yourself: '***Who is*** *on the team list?'*

-------------------------------------------------------------------------------------

## Learning objectives

- To understand spelling patterns.
- To practise using the word **two** in writing.
- To avoid confusing **to**, **too** and **two**.

# Two

## Activity (Answers page 66)

Using the words below, complete the following questions:

**1** What group of letters can you find in common in all the following words?

**2** In which of these words can you hear the **w** when the word is spoken?

**3** Choose two or three of these words (except the word **two**) and write a dictionary definition that includes the word two.

| twelve | twenty | twice | twin | two |
|---|---|---|---|---|

Grammar Matters Too Teacher Resource File © Pearson Education Ltd

# Section 7   APPLYING YOUR LEARNING

## Reading task

Read the following advertisement for the visitor centre at a hydroelectric power station in North Wales. Then complete the task that follows.

### Nature at its most powerful!

*Electric Mountain*

VISITOR CENTRE

*Take the bus underground to see how one of Europe's largest man-made caverns produces electricity.*

A truly electrifying experience for all the family!

Uniquely located in the heart of beautiful Snowdonia, the Electric Mountain Visitor Centre is the gateway to your journey underground to visit one of Europe's largest man-made caverns. Here the most powerful elements of nature have been harnessed by human ingenuity to work together to produce electricity. Our guided tours tell the story of a remarkable achievement of skill, engineering and endeavour. A story that will fascinate and intrigue all the family.

**Task** (Answers page 66)

Using the list of grammatical terms in the box below, fill in the blanks in the following.

The author uses two _____ _____ in the first few lines. These help to add emphasis and emotion to the text. After the heading, the first full _____ starts with the word *Take*. This _____ form of the verb makes the sentence a _____, directing the reader to follow this advice. Used as an _____, the word *electrifying* means 'extremely exciting' as well as linking to *Electric* Mountain. The _____ *Uniquely* at the start of the main paragraph draws attention to the special location of the visitor centre, the whole sentence suggesting it is well worth visiting the area anyway. The _____ _____ *your* in the first sentence of the main paragraph makes it seem as if the writer is addressing you, the reader, directly. It implies you are definitely going to make this journey underground.

Using the _____ *largest* gives the impression that this is the most extensive man-made cavern in Europe, but the _____ *one* in *one of* reveals that it almost certainly is not the largest of all. The set of three _____ _____ in the last but one sentence, *skill, engineering* and *endeavour*, helps to emphasise just how much human talent and effort have gone into the construction of this power station. In the last sentence, the _____ *fascinate* and *intrigue* suggest that 'all the family' will be involved and strongly interested in a visit, encouraging the reader to make a definite decision and commitment to make that visit.

> **Grammatical terms** (each term is used once)
> abstract nouns     adjective     adverb     directive
> exclamation marks     imperative     possessive determiner     pronoun
> sentence     superlative     verbs

# Section 7   APPLYING YOUR LEARNING

## Writing task

(Answers pages 66–67)

Write ten directives advising other students on how they can improve their writing by using some of the techniques covered in this book.

Directives are sentences that instruct someone to do something. For example:

*Vary the position of adverbs in your sentences by ...*

You can choose from the suggested words in the table below or use your own, but you should aim to use about ten words from the *middle* column.

| Verb in imperative form | Grammatical term | Other terms |
|---|---|---|
| avoid | adjective | balance |
| choose |     comparative | impact |
| extend |     superlative | interest |
| improve | adverb | mixture |
| increase | preposition | number |
| select | noun | pattern |
| use |     count | place |
| vary |     non-count | position |
| widen | verb | punctuation |
| |     infinitive | range |
| |     imperative | spelling |
| |     participle | type |
| | prefix | variety |
| | suffix | vocabulary |
| | sentence | |
| |     exclamation | |
| |     statement | |
| |     question | |
| |     directive | |
| |     simple | |
| |     compound | |
| |     complex | |
| | connective | |

Now select the top three pieces of advice that you would give to *yourself* to improve the quality of your own writing.

# Part C   Answers to Additional activities
## Section 1: Words and phrases
## Prefixes, stems and suffixes

### Activity 1 (Page 25)

| verb + *-able* = adjective | adjective + *-ly* = adverb | adjective + *-ness* = noun |
|---|---|---|
| acceptable | amazingly | boldness |
| achieveable | boldly | carefulness |
| agreeable | carefully | directness |
| believeable | directly | fairness |
| changeable | extremely | faithfulness |
| laughable | fairly | happiness |
| reasonable | faithfully | inquisitiveness |
| reliable | happily | liveliness |
| remarkable | immediately | nervousness |
| valueable | inquisitively | politeness |
| (rely *y to i*) | mainly | tiredness |
| | nervously | wholeness |
| | ominously | (happy *y to i*) |
| | physically | (lively *y to i*) |
| | politely | |
| | successfully | |
| | tiredly | |
| | unusually | |
| | wholely | |
| | (happy *y to i*) | |

### Activity 2 (Page 25)

| inter-<br>Definition: between | mis-<br>Definition: bad, badly | pre-<br>Definition: before |
|---|---|---|
| Intercity | misbehave | prefix |
| interconnect | miscast | preheat |
| interface | misfortune | prehistoric |
| interlink | misinform | preset |
| international | miskick | preview |
| Internet | mislead | prewar |
| interstate | misprint | |

# Nouns

## Activity 2 (Page 26)

The most likely word class for a similar activity would be verbs, as verbs can indicate the kinds of activity associated with a particular noun.

e.g. *to kick, to score, to tackle*

Adjectives and adverbs *without the words they modify* tend to be far less topic specific.

## Activity 3 (Page 27)

| Type | Singular | Plural | Rule | Suffix |
|---|---|---|---|---|
| 1a | book<br>dream<br>house<br>writer | books<br>dreams<br>houses<br>writers | For most nouns, just add -*s*.<br>(1) | **-s** |
| 1b | belief<br>chief<br>proof<br>roof<br>knife<br>life<br>wife | beliefs<br>chiefs<br>proofs<br>roofs<br>knives<br>lives<br>wives | For some nouns ending in *f*, just add -*s*. For nouns ending in *fe*, change the *f* to *v* before adding -*s*.<br>(5) | |
| 1c | kilo<br>photo<br>radio<br>video<br>zero | kilos<br>photos<br>radios<br>videos<br>zeros | For some nouns ending in *o*, especially shortened nouns, just add -*s*.<br>(6) | |
| 2a | baby<br>lady<br>story<br>worry | babies<br>ladies<br>stories<br>worries | For nouns ending in a consonant + y, change the *y* to *i* before adding -*es*.<br>(2) | **-es** |
| 2b | calf<br>half<br>leaf<br>loaf<br>thief | calves<br>halves<br>leaves<br>loaves<br>thieves | For some nouns ending in *f*, change the *f* to *v* before adding -*es*.<br>(4) | |
| 2c | hero<br>mosquito<br>potato<br>tomato | heroes<br>mosquitoes<br>potatoes<br>tomatoes | For some nouns ending in *o*, just add -*es*.<br>(7) | |
| 2d | branch<br>brush<br>bus<br>guess<br>hoax<br>quiz | branches<br>brushes<br>buses<br>guesses<br>hoaxes<br>quizzes | For nouns ending in *ch, sh, s, ss, x, z* just add -*es*.<br>(3) | |

**Note:** *quiz* to *quizzes* gains an extra z.

# Pronouns

## Activity (Page 28)

Sample answers:

<u>Those expensive running shoes in the shop</u> have been sold. (<u>They</u> have been sold.)

<u>Ann's exciting adventure holiday in China</u> started yesterday. (<u>It</u> started yesterday.)

The ICT department bought <u>two lap-top computers with extra features</u>. (The ICT department bought <u>them</u>.)

<u>David's mountain bicycle which I borrowed</u> is the best I've ever tried. (<u>It</u> is the best I've ever tried.)

<u>All the best football games on television</u> are on just one channel. (<u>They</u> are on just one channel.)

**Note:** <u>Ann's exciting adventure holiday</u> started in China yesterday; in this case *in China* is an adverbial.

# Adjectives

## Activity 1 (Page 29)

| | | |
|---|---|---|
| *tall* → | man | ← *taller* |
| *wiry* → | *black* → | hair |
| *speckled* → | *pink* → | surface |
| trousers | ← *thick* | ← *heavy* |
| *hottest* → | | day |
| *thick* → | *heavy* → | glasses |
| glasses | ← *enormous* | |
| *bright* → | *silver* → | frames |
| *two* → | *different* → | sorts |

## Activity 2 (Page 30)

**1**

| Original adjective | Comparative | Superlative |
|---|---|---|
| bad | worse | worst |
| few | fewer | fewest |
| good | better | best |
| little | less | least |
| many/much | more | most |

**2**

| Lowest degree | Lower degree | Same degree | Higher degree (comparative) | Highest degree (superlative) |
|---|---|---|---|---|
| least attractive | less attractive | as attractive as | more attractive | most attractive |
| least beautiful | less beautiful | as beautiful as | more beautiful | most beautiful |
| least cheap | less cheap | as cheap as | cheaper | cheapest |
| least effective | less effective | as effective as | more effective | most effective |
| least exciting | less exciting | as exciting as | more exciting | most exciting |
| least successful | less successful | as successful as | more successful | most successful |
| least tasty | less tasty | as tasty as | more tasty/ tastier | most tasty/ tastiest |

# Verbs

## Activity 1 (Page 31)

This section as a whole will demonstrate there are more than 200 ways to use the verb *to speak*.

### Step 1

Three minutes is probably the maximum for the paired discussion part of this activity. Short sharp feedback should establish the options:

***To speak***

- *I/you* (singular)/*we*/*you* (plural)/*they* **speak**
- *he/she/it* **speaks**
- *I/you/he/she/it/we/you/they* **spoke**

### Step 2

From this point onwards, permutations multiply exponentially! For the sake of sanity, it is probably wise to restrict most students to first person only: *I am speaking, I was speaking,* etc.

- *I am; you are; he is; she is; it is; we are; you are; they are* **speaking** (8)
- *am speaking               are speaking*
- *I was; you were; he/she/it was; we were; you were; they were* **speaking** (8)
- *was speaking               were speaking*
- *I am; you are; he/she/it is; we are; you are; they are* **being spoken to** (8)
- *am being spoken* (to)     *are being spoken* (to)
- *I was; you were; he/she/it was/we were; you were/they were,* etc. **spoken to** (8)
- *was spoken* (to)               *were spoken* (to)
- *I was; you were; he/she/it was; we were; you were/they were,* etc. **being spoken to** (8)
- *was being spoken* (to)       *were being spoken* (to)

### Step 3

- *I have spoken to the whole class.* (*She has,* etc.) (8)
  *have spoken               has spoken*
- *Having spoken to my parents ...* (1)
  *Having spoken*
- *I had; you had; he/she/it had; we had; you had* **spoken** ... (8)
  *had spoken*

### Step 4

- *I do; you do; he/she/it does; we do; you do; they do* **speak clearly**. (8)
  *do speak     does speak*
- *I did; you did; he/she/it did; we did; you did; they did* **speak out of turn**. (8)
  *did speak*

### Step 5

- I *can speak*
- I *could speak*
- I *may speak*
- I *might speak*
- I *must speak*

- I *ought to speak*
- I *shall speak*
- I *should speak*
- I *will speak*

**Step 6**

- I *could have spoken.* (8)
- I *have been speaking* to the whole class. (*She has*, etc.) (8)
- I *have been spoken to* by my boss. (*She has*, etc.) (8)
- I *may be speaking* out of turn. (8)
- I *may have spoken* out of turn. (8)
- I *might be speaking* out of turn. (8)
- I *might have been speaking* out of turn. (8)
- I *might have spoken* out of turn. (8)
- I *must be speaking* too loud. (8)
- I *must have been speaking* too loudly. (8)
- I *must have spoken* at some point. (8)
- I *ought to be speaking* more. (8)
- I *ought to have spoken.* (8)
- I *should be speaking* less. (8)
- I *should have been speaking* more sensibly. (8)
- I *should have spoken.* (8)
- I *will be speaking* more confidently in future. (8)

**Note:** Modal auxiliary verbs come before other auxiliary verbs.

## Activity 2 (Page 33)

Chips hissed and bubbled as they were dragged out of the fryer, oil draining off them like a waterfall. Customers entered and left in a constant cycle, pushing and jostling in the queue. Fish crackled, newspaper rustled, gravy sloshed and fat dripped. Bubbles gasped for air as they rose from under the chips. The potato machine gargled as it spat out another batch. The till chimed as it was slammed shut, gulping as it swallowed more money.

**Possible ways to improve**

- Perhaps 'entered' and 'left' are the most predictable verbs. Students should discuss how far they feel any improvements make the text as a whole sound more effective.
- Don't start every sentence with a noun. Students could be asked how they could move the verb to increase variety.

e.g. *Gasping for air, bubbles rose from under the chips.*

## Activity 3 (Page 34)

| | Sentence example | Auxiliary verb before main verb? | Participle form? | Standard English? |
|---|---|---|---|---|
| **1** | He had written it himself. | ✓ had | ✓ written | Yes |
| **2** | She did the crossword before breakfast. | ✗ | ✗ | Yes |
| **3** | The newspaper is wrote in a different way. | ✓ is | ✗ | No |

|   | Sentence example | Auxiliary verb before main verb? | Participle form? | Standard English? |
|---|------------------|----------------------------------|------------------|-------------------|
| **4** | She done her homework quickly. | ✗ | ✓ done | No |
| **5** | They had already gone out. | ✓ had | ✓ gone | Yes |

**Note:** You need an auxiliary verb with a participle form.
You should not combine an auxiliary verb with a past form.

# Adverbs

### Activity 1 (Page 35)

**1**   *quickly* is modifying the verb *do*. **Adverbs** modify verbs (and other adverbs); **adjectives** don't modify verbs.

**2**   *blindly* is modifying the verb *walking*. **Adverbs** modify verbs (and other adverbs); **adjectives** don't modify verbs.

**3**   It becomes boring if the adverb is always placed in the same position. More variety and interest can be generated by deliberately choosing different positions for the adverb – at the start of the sentence, before and after the verb, etc.

### Activity 2 (Page 35)

**A**   suspiciously + adjective *rusty*

**B**   casually + verb *waved*

**C**   never even + verb *been*

**D**   verb *been* + before

**E**   Honestly + verb *is*

**F**   Besides = sentence connector

**G**   verb *did* + exactly

**H**   silently + verb *urged*

**I**   Finally + verb *crept up*

**J**   verb *rocked* + slightly

**K**   comfortably + -*ing* participle *missing*

For most students, A, B, E, G, H, I, J and K will be sufficient to find and analyse.

### Activity 3 (Page 36)

| **Where?** | in Paris; to the stadium |
|------------|--------------------------|
| **When?** | At the weekend; after midnight |
| **How long?** | For a fortnight; about 10 metres long |
| **How often?** | Every other Saturday; each week |
| **How?** | by train; by hand |
| **Why?** | Because of the rain; for fun |
| **With whom?** | with a group of friends; on our own |

# Section 2 | SENTENCES

## Checking agreement

**Activity** (Page 39)

<u>It</u>'s easy to identify with Zinny in this warm and funny story about the confusion of growing up and the need to find a true sense of yourself. <u>Her rumbustious family</u>, with its three boys and four girls, lives in a rambling farm with their aunt and uncle next door. For Zinny, <u>Uncle Nate's and Aunt Jessie's house</u> has always been a sanctuary where she can talk and be heard, something she finds hard in her own home. But when her beloved Auntie Jessie dies unexpectedly, <u>Zinny</u> finds it hard to get her bearings. <u>Her thoughts</u> are like tangled spaghetti and she cannot put them back in order.

## Object, Complement and Adverbial

**Activity 1** (Page 40)

**1**    Unwrap <u>all the components</u> and lay <u>them</u> out all over the floor.

**2**    Count <u>all the pieces</u> and check <u>them</u>.

**3**    Line up <u>the ready-drilled screw-holes</u> and use <u>the screws provided</u>.

**4**    Fit <u>the screws provided</u> into the ready-drilled holes.

**5**    Take <u>one of the longest planks (uprights)</u> and fix <u>the top plank</u> to it.

**6**    Fix <u>the second upright</u> to the top of the bookcase.

**7**    Fix <u>the shelf supports</u> into the ready-drilled holes in the second upright at the same intervals as the first.

**8**    Fit <u>the shelves</u>.

**9**    Stand <u>the bookcase</u> in the desired location.

**Note:** Only the direct objects of the verbs have been underlined.

# Section 3    BUILDING    SENTENCES

## Building simple sentences

### Activity (Page 41)

**Positives**

Creates a sense of atmosphere.

Describes emotions as well as events.

Uses dynamic verbs such as *crashed, trapped, forced, grabbed*.

**Problems**

Too many sentences start with 'I'.

The pattern of sentences is too repetitive.

There needs to be a variety of simple, compound and complex sentences.

## Compound sentences

### Activity (Page 42)

**Positives**

More variety in sentence structure than previous version.

The use of *but* and *or* clearly signals to the reader the logic of the links between different parts of a sentence.

Some simple sentences now have a more dramatic effect as they are different: *I felt sick with fear.*

**Problems**

Using only *and*, *but* and *or* limits the possible alternatives.

Too many sentences still start with 'I'.

The pattern of subject + verb becomes repetitive.

## Connectives

### Activity (Page 42)

**a**   This event comes around once a year so I have a year to recover from it.
I have a year to recover from this event as it comes around once a year.
As this event comes around once a year, I have a year to recover from it.

**b**   If you have a family then the beach scene would appeal to you, whereas if you are single then the white-water rafting picture might appeal to you.
If you are single then the white-water rafting picture might appeal to you, whereas if you have a family then the beach scene would appeal to you.

**c**   He was always willing to help since I was his favourite nephew.
I was his favourite nephew so he was always willing to help.
Because I was his favourite nephew, he was always willing to help.

Grammar Matters Too Teacher Resource File © Pearson Education Ltd

# Complex sentences

## Activity (Page 43)

### Positives

A mixture of simple, compound and complex sentences adds to the interest.
Complex sentences are formed in two different ways to add to the variety.
The sentences start in a variety of ways.

### Sample advice

Start your sentences in a variety of ways.
Use a variety of connectives to show the logical links between different parts of your sentences.
Use a careful combination of simple, compound and complex sentences to achieve variety.
You can use short, simple sentences to heighten tension at the most dramatic moment in a story, or to add emphasis in a persuasive piece of writing.

# Section 4   PARAGRAPHS AND WHOLE TEXTS

## Activity (Page 44)

1   Possible sequence of paragraphs (But note: students may decide to deliberately withhold certain information for particular effects, and this may well change the order details are presented.)

- age
- appearance
- height
- eye/hair colour
- hair style
- clothing for different purposes
- typical footwear
- favourite books/music/sport
- favourite possession
- habits
- hobbies
- typical leisure time activities
- friendship groups
- achievements
- overall character/personality

# Section 5   PUNCTUATION

# Capital letters

## Activity (Page 45)

| | | | |
|---|---|---|---|
| **1** | D | **3** | B |
| **2** | C | **4** | A |

# Question marks

**Activity** (Page 45)

**1**    Not rhetorical.

**2**    Rhetorical expecting no as an answer.

**3**    Rhetorical expecting no answer (but as part of an advertisement encouraging the reader to buy a pair).

**4**    Not rhetorical.

**5**    Rhetorical expecting yes as an answer.

**Note:**

Rhetorical questions framed as a negative usually expect the answer yes.

Rhetorical questions framed as a positive usually expect the answer no.

# Commas

**Activity** (Page 46)

**a**    A megabyte equals 1,048,576 bytes. *G*

**b**    If it doesn't rain, we could go to the park. *C*

**c**    Elaine asked, 'Where are we going?' *E*

**d**    She wore a beautiful, new, sparkly, black dress. *B*

**e**    Carefully, he opened the door. *F*

**f**    The drivers, who knew about the floods, took another route. *D*

**g**    On holiday we visited towns in France, Spain, Portugal and Italy. *A*

# Apostrophes

**Activity 1** (Page 47)

The label 'possessive apostrophe' fits **e** very well, but does not work so well for some of the other examples.

**Activity 2** (Page 47)

**a**    An evening in winte**r**.          A winte**r**'s evening.

**b**    The work of each othe**r**.         Each othe**r**'s work.

**c**    The evening for parent**s**.        Parent**s**' evening.

**d**    The trilogy by Philip Pullma**n**.   Philip Pullma**n**'s trilogy.

**e**    The gym for the gir**ls**.           The gir**ls**' gym.

**f**    The decision by the refere**e**.     The refere**e**'s decision.

Always place the 'apostrophe of possession' *immediately after the last letter of the full version.*

## Activity 3 (Page 48)

**a**    Some OAPs walk through the doors.

**b**    Sweaty, hot and bothered employees try to do their best in pleasing customers.

**Note:** For initials, etc. use a combination of upper case and lower case: OAPs, JCBs, CDs, DOs and DON'Ts. Never use an apostrophe simply because the noun is in the plural.

# Colons

## Activity (Page 49)

**a**    She decided not to argue: the holiday was already booked. *B*

**b**    To make scrambled eggs you need: milk, butter and eggs. *A*

**c**    As the train manager said: driving the train is only half the story. *C*

# Semicolons

## Activity (Page 50)

**a**    I like pasta; she likes curry. *C*

**b**    She loves ballet and tap dancing; running and cycling; and all sorts of reading. *A*

**c**    The bus was late; I got to school late; the day had started badly. *B*

# Speech marks/inverted commas

## Activity (Page 51)

| | Instructions | Example |
|---|---|---|
| **1** | Put " at the start of any words that are spoken. | "Mum, Mum, let's go on Megaphobia first |
| **2** | There must be a punctuation mark inside the closing inverted commas. ( , . ! or ?) | "Mum, Mum, let's go on Megaphobia first**,**" screamed Samuel. |
| **3** | Put " at end of any words that are spoken. | "Mum, Mum, let's go on Megaphobia first**,**" |
| **4** | Start a new line for a new speaker. | "Mum, Mum, let's go on Megaphobia first," screamed Samuel.<br>    "No – the pirate ship Mum," yelled Lucy. |
| **5** | f speech starts after the beginning of a sentence, put a comma just before it starts. | Mum tried to calm them by saying**,** "It's all right, we'll go on both …" |
| **6** | The speech should start with a capital letter … but … | Mum tried to calm them by saying, "**It's** all right, we'll go on both …" |
| **7** | … if a speech carries on for a second time within a sentence, use lower case at the start (except for proper nouns, etc.). | "Perhaps," she replied, "**if** you stop shouting and interrupting!" |

# Section 6   COMMON   ERRORS

## Who's/Whose

**Activity** (Page 52)

**1** Who *has* been sleeping in my bed?

**3** Who *is* in the kitchen?

**4** Who *is* going to take you home?

**5** Who *has* eaten the last chocolate?

## Two

**Activity** (Page 52)

**1** *tw*

**2** twelve, twenty, twice, twin

# Section 7   APPLYING YOUR   LEARNING

## Reading task

**Task** (Page 53)

The author uses two **exclamation marks** in the first few lines. These help to add emphasis and emotion to the text. After the heading, the first full **sentence** starts with the word *Take*. This **imperative** form of the verb makes the sentence a **directive**, directing the reader to follow this advice. Used as an **adjective**, the word *electrifying* means 'extremely exciting' as well as linking to *Electric* Mountain. The **adverb** *Uniquely* at the start of the main paragraph draws attention to the special location of the visitor centre, the whole sentence suggesting it is well worth visiting the area anyway. The **possessive determiner** *your* in the first sentence of the main paragraph makes it seem as if the writer is addressing you, the reader, directly. It implies you are definitely going to make this journey underground.

Using the **superlative** *largest* gives the impression that this is the most extensive man-made cavern in Europe, but the **pronoun** *one* in *one of* reveals that it almost certainly is not the largest of all. The set of three **abstract nouns** in the last but one sentence, *skill*, *engineering* and *endeavour*, help to emphasise just how much human talent and effort have gone into the construction of this power station. In the last sentence, the **verbs** *fascinate* and *intrigue* suggest that 'all the family' will be involved and strongly interested in a visit, encouraging the reader to make a definite decision and commitment to make that visit.

## Writing task

**Task** (Page 54)

**Sample suggestions**

**1** Choose sentences that are *statements* most of the time, but make a careful use of *exclamations* and *questions* when appropriate.

**2** Improve your spelling by understanding how words are formed using *prefixes* and *suffixes*.

**3** Increase the power of your writing by deliberately choosing verbs that have a particular impact when appropriate.

**4** Increase your choices when using adjectives by using *comparisons* at the same, lower and higher levels (least, less, as … as, more, most) as well as using the adjective in its base form.

**5**   Make use of *connectives* to extend and vary your sentence patterns.

**6**   Use a range of prepositions in various positions in your sentences to increase the variety of your writing, especially about places.

**7**   Use a variety of sentence structures, including *simple* sentences, *compound* sentences and *complex* sentences to add interest to your writing.

**8**   Use *directives* to tell people what to do or what to think!

**9**   Vary the number and position of adjectives in your sentences.

**10**   Vary the position of adverbs in your sentences, for example by placing them at the start of the sentence, *before* the verb and *after* the verb.

# Part D Additional resources
## Self-assessment table

Give yourself a rating on some of these statements.

**1** = I need to do more to build my confidence here.

**2** = I am beginning to be successful here.

**3** = I am fairly confident in this area.

**4** = I am confident in this area.

| Statement | Rating (1–4) |
|---|---|
| I know what a prefix is and can explain what meaning some prefixes have. | |
| I know what a suffix is and can explain what meaning some suffixes have. | |
| In my writing I deliberately choose the noun I think works best. | |
| I know when to use the subject pronoun (e.g. *I*) and when to use the object pronoun (e.g. *me*), and can explain how I know. | |
| In my writing I deliberately choose the adjective I think works best. | |
| I deliberately choose one, two or three adjectives (or none); I place adjectives before and after the noun to achieve variety and different effects. | |
| I deliberately choose comparative and superlative adjectives when appropriate. | |
| In my writing I deliberately choose the verb I think works best. | |
| I can use a range of auxiliary verbs effectively, and make appropriate use of the infinitive, the imperative and *-ing/-ed* participles in my writing. | |
| In my writing I deliberately choose the adverb I think works best. | |
| I use adverbs at various points in the sentence to achieve variety and different effects. | |
| I can identify the main verb in a sentence. | |
| I can tell when a group of words makes complete sense. | |
| I use a variety of sentences in my writing including: simple, compound, complex; short, long; statements, exclamations, questions, directives. | |
| I use a wide variety of connectives in forming complex sentences, and can change the word order for particular effects. | |
| I can use a full range of punctuation marks and explain why I am using a particular punctuation mark. | |
| I have a range of strategies for checking my spelling. | |

# True or false grammar quiz

## Prefixes and suffixes

**True or false?**

**1**   A referee should always be disinterested.

## Nouns

**True or false?**

**2**   *A* and *the* can be used in sentences with all nouns.
e.g. I like to read *a book* in bed. I liked *the book*.

**3**   All nouns have a singular and plural form.
e.g. *one book, two books*

## Pronouns

**True or false?**

**4**   You should always say and write *you and I* rather than *you and me*.

**5**   There are two forms of the first person pronoun: *I* and *me*.

## Adjectives

**True or false?**

**6**   Adjectives only modify (affect the meaning of) **nouns**.

**7**   No adjectives in the English language have separate masculine and feminine forms.

## Verbs

**True or false?**

**8**   A verb is a *doing* word.

**9**   Verbs in the English language have three tenses: past, present and future.

## Adverbs

**True or false?**

**10**   An adverb only modifies (affects the meaning of) a verb.

**11**   Adverbs always come after the verb.
e.g. He spoke *quietly*.

**12**   You shouldn't split an infinitive with an adverb – I'm going **to** *completely* **change** my exercise routine.

**13**   Adverbs always end in *-ly*.

## Prepositions

**True or false?**

**14**   You should not end a sentence with a preposition.

**15**   A preposition always comes just before a noun.

# True or false grammar quiz answers

## Prefixes and suffixes

**1**   True
*interested* can mean *having an emotional involvement*, even leading to favouritism ... the opposite of this is **dis**interested – not showing favouritism or bias, impartial. *interested* can also mean *showing attention* ... the opposite of this is **un**interested – not showing any attention.

## Nouns

**2**   False
*A* and *the* can be used in sentences with most countable nouns. 'The' can be used in most sentences with most nouns, but usually not proper nouns.

**3**   False
Countable nouns usually have a singular and plural form. There are exceptions such as *sheep* where the singular and plural forms are the same. Non-count nouns do not change.

## Pronouns

**4**   False
Use *You and I* as the subject of the sentence, *you and me* for the object of the sentence. You also need to use *you and me* after a preposition: *They'll soon come to you and me for advice.* (Compare *They'll soon come to **me** for advice.*)

**5**   False
There are five versions: *I, me, my, mine, myself.*

## Adjectives

**6**   True

**7**   False
For example, *blond* when referring to males and *blonde* when referring to females.

## Verbs

**8**   False; it isn't always. Verbs such as *to seem, to be, to know* do not fit this description.

**9**   False
There is a *present* form of the verb and a *past* form of the verb, but no *future* form of the verb. In English, future time is expressed in a variety of ways, including by using the modal auxiliary verb 'will'.

## Adverbs

**10**   False
For example, adverbs can intensify other adverbs: **extremely** quickly, **very** unusually. They can also modify adjectives, for example: **extremely** cold.

**11**   False
Adverbs can be placed in a variety of positions in the sentence, including at the start and before the verb. *He quietly informed the class of his decision.*

**12**   False
Modern experts on grammar say there is no rule against splitting the infinitive, and that being able to split the infinitive adds to the range of ways you can convey your exact meaning. However, be warned: some people believe the rule that says you *shouldn't* split infinitives exists!

**13**   False
Many adverbs do not end in *-ly*, e.g. *here* and *far*.

## Prepositions

**14**   False
*Where shall I send it to?* would become *Whither shall I send it? What are you thinking of?* would become *Of what are you thinking? That's the person I was referring to.* would become *That's the person to whom I was referring.* These alternatives sound unnatural and over-formal.

**15**   False
For example, prepositions are very commonly used in phrasal verbs such as *talk about, come on, shut up*.

# Nouns fact sheet

## Examples of nouns in each category

| Proper | Common | | | |
|---|---|---|---|---|
| | concrete | | | abstract |
| | person | place | thing | |
| Amanda | boy | classroom | door | idea |
| London | girl | school | table | sunshine |
| Rolex | man | house | computer | happiness |
| Corgi | woman | supermarket | football (the ball) | problem |
| Vauxhall | teacher | playing field | team | dream |
| New Zealand | student | gymnasium | newspaper | football (the game) |
| September | dramatist | bedroom | book | success |
| Monday | author | concert hall | hair | malaria |

| Countable | | | Uncountable | |
|---|---|---|---|---|
| a/the | boy | boys | sugar | the sugar |
| a/the | girl | girls | electricity | the electricity |
| a/the | man | men | money | the money |
| a/the | house | houses | happiness | the happiness |
| a/the | computer | computers | stamina | the stamina |
| a/the | dream | dreams | malaria | the malaria |
| an/the | idea | ideas | sunshine | the sunshine |
| a/the | party | parties | future | the future |

# Pronouns and possessive determiners fact sheet

| | Subject pronoun | Object pronoun | Possessive pronoun | Reflexive pronoun | Possessive determiner |
|---|---|---|---|---|---|
| 1st person singular | I<br>*I agreed to do it.* | me<br>*It came towards* **me**. | mine<br>*That phone is* **mine**. | myself<br>*I wrote it* **myself**. | my<br>**My** *best friend is …* |
| 2nd person singular | you | you | yours | yourself | your |
| 3rd person singular | he<br>she<br>it | him<br>her<br>it | his<br>hers<br>its<br>**Its** *(remote control) has gone missing.* | himself<br>herself<br>itself | his<br>her<br>its<br>**Its** *fur keeps the warmth in.* |
| | anybody, anyone, anything, everybody, everyone, everything, nobody, no one, nothing, somebody, someone, something | | | | |
| 1st person plural | we | us | ours | ourselves | our |
| 2nd person plural | you | you | yours | yourselves | your |
| 3rd person plural | they | them | theirs | themselves | their |
| (relative pronoun) | who | whom *(formal)*<br>who *(less formal)*<br>*To whom am I speaking?* | whose<br>*Whose book is this?* | | |

## Guidance

The **subject** form is used when the pronoun is acting as the subject:
*I* phoned home.    ***She*** *phoned home.*    ***We*** *phoned home.*

The **object** form is used when the pronoun is acting as the object:
*The company phoned* **me**.    *The company phoned* **her**.    *The company phoned* **us**.

The **object** form is also used when the pronoun comes after a preposition – in this case the preposition *to*:
*The teacher spoke* <u>to</u> **me**.    *The teacher spoke* <u>to</u> **her**.    *The teacher spoke* <u>to</u> **us**.

Reflexive pronouns are used in sentences such as:
*I hurt* **myself**.    *Enjoy* **yourselves***!*

There are also possessive determiners: **my    your    his    her    its    our    their**.
As in: **my** *book*    **your** *choice*    **their** *decision*

# Prepositions fact sheet

| Time | Place | Movement | Other |
|------|-------|----------|-------|
| about | above | across | by (car) |
| before | among | along | except |
| during | at | back to | of |
| for | behind | down | unlike |
| from | below | from | with |
| on | beneath | into | without (a cloud) |
| past (bedtime) | beside | off | |
| throughout (the film) | between | onto | |
| to | beyond | out of | |
| unt l | by | over | |
| within (a week) | in | past | |
| | in front of | round (the runr ing | |
| | inside | track) | |
| | near | through | |
| | next to | to | |
| | on | towards | |
| | opposite (the station) | under | |
| | outside | up | |
| | under | | |
| | underneath | | |
| | within (sight) | | |

**Note:** Some prepositions can be used in more than one category.

# Conjunctions/Connectives fact sheet

| Co-ordinating conjunctions can be used to create compound sentences | |
|---|---|
| and | I went to my bedroom. I played my favourite track. |
| | I went to my bedroom *and* (I) played my favourite track. |
| but | I went to bed. I couldn't get to sleep. |
| | I went to bed *but* (I) couldn't get to sleep. |
| or | You can read a book. You can go to bed. |
| | You can read a book *or* (you can) go to bed. |

| Subordinating conjunctions can be used to create complex sentences | |
|---|---|
| **when?** | |
| after | The most brilliant colours appeared *after* the sun had set. |
| as | She reached the station *as* the train was pulling out. |
| before | I had agreed to make my decision *before* my parents left for work. |
| once | You can go out *once* you have finished. |
| since | I had been training hard *since* the day I had been selected. |
| until | She decided to wait *until* the immediate danger had passed. |
| while | I told him the news *while* he was eating breakfast. |
| **where?** | |
| where | I hid it *where* nobody would think of looking for it. |
| wherever | I went to watch the team *wherever* they were playing. |
| **how?** | |
| by | I raised some extra money *by* doing jobs for my older brother. |
| through | She won the race *through* having extra coaching. |
| **why?** | |
| as | I didn't go *as* it was raining. |
| because | I changed my mind *because* the coach was so persuasive. |
| since | She was even more nervous *since* her friends were watching. |
| so that | The student asked for more time *so that* he could solve the problem. |
| **on condition ...?** | |
| although | We weren't allowed in *although* the game hadn't started. |
| if | The teacher told me I could go *if* my parents agreed. |
| unless | I was warned I couldn't see my favourite programme *unless* I cleaned my bedroom. |

 Grammar Matters Too Teacher Resource File © Pearson Education Ltd